Illinois Central College
Learning Resources Center

SELECTED POEMS

Robert Bly

SELECTED POEMS

I.C.C. LIBRARY

PERENNIAL LIBRARY

HARPER & ROW, PUBLISHERS, New York

Cambridge, Philadelphia, San Francisco, London
Mexico City, São Paulo, Singapore, Sydney

Permissions Acknowledgments appear on page 213.

FIRST EDITION

Designed by Ruth Bornschlegel

Library of Congress Cataloging-in-Publication Data

Bly, Robert.
  Selected poems.

  Includes indexes.
  I. Title.
PS3552.L9A6   1986   811'.54   84-47556
ISBN 0-06-015334-2   86 87 88 89 90 MPC 10 9 8 7 6 5 4 3 2 1
ISBN 0-06-096048-5 (pbk.)   86 87 88 89 90 MPC 10 9 8 7 6 5 4 3 2 1

Contents

Afterthoughts 193

Part One

THE LUTE OF THREE
LOUDNESSES

My first poetry seems to me now to keep out a despair that I couldn't quite bring into the house. Wanting a noble art, I aimed to learn the melodic line the English poets developed, sometimes called "iambic," sometimes "accentual-syllabic." Whatever we call it, the instrument the English poets constructed over centuries with its strings and resonating box makes amazing music. The rhyme, originally a plumlike sweetness natural to sung poems, keeps the poet aware which of the fifty or so main sounds in English he or she is using. Moreover the felt need to care for at least three sorts of intensities of sound keeps the composer aware of higher and lower pitches. The form can conceal pain or reveal it. This instrument, which I'll call the lute of three loudnesses or three melodies, when constructed and played by an experienced musician, produces an intricate and swiftly modulating music, in which we can hear several simultaneous melodies. Sometimes a melody of pitches runs over and above the separate rhythm of loudnesses; and sometimes a third ghostly tune rises above these two. Much sixteenth-century poetry in English, Shakespeare's for example, calls for a pause after the fourth syllable. "That time of year thou mayst in me behold." This pause—here or elsewhere in the line—allows the body to rest, or to turn, or to leap, and is another musical event. When a beginning poet constructs a lute of three melodies and learns to play it, he or she will be able to experience in his own poem the whole history of poetry written on English ground, with the exception of the pre-Norman Germanic poetry.

I wrote my first book entirely on this English instrument, over roughly four years from 1948 to 1952, some of that time spent in New York, some in Cambridge. The other day, walking in the woods, I found I had remembered these lines:

> *and see*
> *The agile companies of April sit*
> *As quaint and graceful as medieval guilds.*

I don't tire of the lines, because their tune of pitches keeps the mind alert. I loved the music so much I could have written such lines for the rest of my life, but something in it didn't fit me. When I wrote of Guadalcanal, or trappers or Mandan Indians, I heard a whisper of Milton. I couldn't solve that problem, and for that reason, I did not try to publish my first book. What I like best in the poems still is their music.

from FOUR SEASONS IN
AMERICAN WOODS

Spring has come; I look up and see
The agile companies of April sit
As quaint and graceful as medieval guilds.
Grouse feathers float away on the still lake.
Summer and reeds; summer and partridge chicks.
Then bees: eaters of honey till their death.
The honey gatherers, coming and going, drive
Their endless honey circles to the hive.

The sedge root in the river lifts and frees,
And blackbirds join in flocks, their duties through.
And now the last autumnal freedom comes,
And Zumbrota acorns drop, sun-pushed as plums,
To half-wild hogs in Carolina trees,
And disappointed bees, with half-gold feet,
Sail home. For me this season is most sweet,
And winter will be stamping of the feet.

The heavy crow, the jay and daw,
Awaken in the wild rice,
And cry the cows upon the straw
To pastures and the timber mice.

Out where the thresher stands, the mole
And cricket gnaw the prison twice.
The gopher dozes in his hole;
Dark turkeys loiter through the pine.

Waters are loose: from Judith and the Larb,
Straining and full, the thick Missouri, choked
With sticks and roots, and high with floating trees,
And spoils of snowfields from the Crazy Hills,
Burns loose earth off. The brown Missouri's mouth
Eats earth a hundred feet below the plains.
At dawn we see the crumbling cliffs at first,
Then horse and rider, then the eastern sky.
At daybreak riders shout from western cliffs.
The buffalo, in herds, come down to drink,
Turn back, and shoulders humping, racket on
Up dust-chewn paths onto the plains of dust;
And I have heard the buffalo stampede
With muffled clatter of colliding horns.
A subtle peril hangs above this land
Like smoke that floats at dawn above dead fires.

The dead in scaffolds float on steady rafts,
Corroding in their sepulchers of air.
At dawn the Osage part their tepee doors,
Cutting their arms and thighs with sharp-edged shells.
The dark-blue buzzard flocks awake on trees
And stretch their black wings toward the sun to dry.
Such are the few details that I have seen.

And there are signs of what will come: the whites
With steel traps hanging, swung from saddle thongs.
The busy whites believe these Sioux and Kaws
And Mandans are not men at all, but beasts:
Some snake-bound beast, regressed, embedded, wound,

Held in damnation, and by death alone
To be released. The Sioux are still and silent
Generally, and I have watched them stand
By ones and twos upon the riverbank,
As still as Hudson's blankets winding them,
While shuttling steamboats, smoking, labor up,
Invading the landscape of their youth and dreams,
Pushed up, they say, by smoke; and they believe
This tribe of whites, like smoke, soon shall return
From where it came. The truth drops out of mind,
As if the pain of action were so great
And life so freezing and Medusa-faced
That, like Medusa's head, it could be held
And not observed, lest its reward be stone.

Now night grows old above this riverboat.
Before I end, I shall include account
Of incident tonight that moved my wonder.
At dusk we tied the ship to trees on shore;
No mortal boat in these night shoals can live.
At first I heard a cry: then shufflings, steps.
The muffled sounds on deckoak overhead
Drew me on deck. The air was chill, and there
I sensed, because these senses here are sharp
And must be, something living and unknown.
To night and north a crowd stared from the boatrail,
Upriver, northward, nightward; a speck of white.
The thing was white: the resonance of night
Returned its whiffs and whistlings on the air.
The frontier men swore in that river thicket,

In ambush like the lizards they're modeled on,
Bristling for war, would be a thresh of Sioux.
And gamblers, nudging the settlers, baiting them:
"Along the river there's some settler's cow!
Maybe a pagan pig, some Poland China,
The settler could not keep inside his crib.
He's free, and terrorizing catfish now."
But Mormons see some robe in that faint white,
An angel of death upon the chill Missouri.
One man believed that there was nothing there,
As the moon is false, and all its light is false.
I felt a fear, as if it were protected.
When the talk died, eight men, and I with them,
Set off and, moving overboard in dark,
With guns, protected by the thunder's noise,
Up the dark stream, toward where the splashes rose,
So armed in case of Sioux, to our surprise
We found a white and wounded Northern Bear,
Shot in that day about the snout and head.
The pure-white bear, not native to these parts,
But to the Horns, or Ranges, born, and shot
That morning, had turned west or south in pain,
And had apparently through these dry plains
Turned west, to lay its burning paws and head
And place its fever-proud and festered flesh
Within the cool Missouri's turbid bed.
I felt as I had once when through a door,
At ten or twelve, I'd seen my mother bathing.
Soon after, clouds of rain drove us indoors,
And lightning; swift rain fell in sheets; such rain

Said to be sudden in these Western lands.
Minutes before it broke, a circling mass
Of split-tail swallows came and then were gone.

The dove returns; it found no resting place;
It was in flight all night above the shaken seas.
Beneath ark eaves
The dove shall magnify the tiger's bed;
Give the dove peace.
The split-tail swallows leave the sill at dawn;
At dusk, blue swallows shall return.
On the third day the crow shall fly;
The crow, the crow, the spider-colored crow,
The crow shall find new mud to walk upon.

Part Two

Poems from

THE ROAD OF
POVERTY AND DEATH

The early poems I wrote were musical, but the "I" in them had no weight. I lived for several years in various parts of New York City, longing for "the depths," by which I meant the fruitful depths. I was already underground, but in a solitary dry well, not a depth. The poem "Schoolcraft's Diary" describes a man who emerges from his room in the hold to observe a white bear wounded in the head; I felt a wound also in the body. Most people I knew seemed to do all right, but in solitude I sank as if through one geological layer after another, past conglomerate stones, past Eros, past family affections, past even ordinary conversation, though even while I sank I knew that this depressed state was not private to me. What some old Germanic stories call the hostile mountain spirit —critical judgment—had done his work well. I lived in small dark rooms, and that loneliness made clear to me my interior homelessness, my lack of respect for myself, and my interior starvation.

And I couldn't write about it, which was worse. I would set down a few lines and fall into silence, and even those lines would disappear from the paper a few minutes later. I managed to finish only five or six poems in three years. I saw the estrangement as a story: a man lives in a modern city, aware of a primitive woman bent over ground corn somewhere miles away, and though he is married to her, he has no living connection with her.

Yet the misery had its own justice, because I was living my own life, and not someone else's. The stump of misery occasionally puts out a radiant sprig. After a year and a half of solitude, I experienced a subtle gift, and my serious poetry began.

In New York and Cambridge I wrote a small book, *The Road of Poverty and Death*, whose title I took from the third section of Rilke's *Das Stundenbuch*. I did not publish the book, but drew poems from it when I composed *The Light Around the Body* fourteen years later.

THE FIRE OF DESPAIR HAS BEEN
OUR SAVIOR

Today, autumn.
Heaven's roots are still.
Finch's castle, ruin of leaves, how quickly
We see spring coming in your black branches!
Not like the Middle Ages! Then iron ringing iron
At dawn, chill wringing
The grass, clatter of saddles,
The long rides out of cold stone
Into the chill air sobered by the hidden joy of crows.

Or the Ice Age!
Another child dead,
Turning bone stacks for bones, sleeves of snow blowing
Down from above, no tracks in the snow, in agony
Man cried out—like the mad hog, pierced, again,
Again, by teeth-spears, who
Grew his horny skin
From sheer despair—instants
Finally leading out of the snowbound valley.

Today, autumn.
But I cannot find
The way to winter: all clues vanished, hidden
By spring and fall, leaving a still sky
Here, a dusk there, a dry cornleaf in a field.
I sink and don't sink,
In agony, as when a ship
Miles from sober land goes down,
Where what is left and what goes down both bring
    despair.

There is a joyful night in which we lose
Everything, and drift
Like a radish
Rising and falling, and the ocean
At last throws us into the ocean,
And in the ocean we are sinking
As if floating on darkness.
The body rages
And drives itself, disappearing in smoke,
Walks in large cities late at night,
Or reading the Bible in Christian Science windows,
Or reading a history of Bougainville.
Then the images appear:
Images of death,
Images of the body shaken in the grave,
And the graves filled with sea water.
Fires in the sea,
The ships smoldering like bodies;
Images of wasted life,
Life lost, imagination ruined,
The house fallen,
The gold sticks broken.
Then shall the talkative be silent
And the dumb shall speak.

A HOME IN DARK GRASS

In the deep fall, terror increases,
And we find lions on the seashore—
Nothing to fear.
The wind rises; water is born,
Spreading white tomb-clothes on a rocky shore,
Drawing us up
From the bed of the land.

It is not our job to remain unbroken.
Our task is to lose our leaves
And be born again, as trees
Draw up from the great roots.
So men captured by the Moors
Wake in the detached ocean
Air, living a second life.

To learn of poverty and rags,
To taste the weed of Dillinger,
And swim in the sea,
Not always walking on dry land,
And, dancing, find in the trees a savior,
A home in dark grass,
And nourishment in death.

A MAN WRITES TO A PART OF HIMSELF

What cave are you in, hiding, rained on?
Like a wife, starving, without care,
Water dripping from your head, bent
Over ground corn . . .

You raise your face into the rain
That drives over the valley—
Forgive me, your husband,
On the streets of a distant city, laughing,
With many appointments,
Though at night going also
To a bare room, a room of poverty,
To sleep beside a bare pitcher and basin
In a room with no heat—

Which of us two then is the worse off?
And how did this separation come about?

ON A FERRY ACROSS
CHESAPEAKE BAY

On the orchard of the sea far out are whitecaps,
Water that answers questions no one has asked,
Silently speaking the grave's rejoinders.
Having accomplished nothing, I am traveling somewhere
    else.
Oh deep green sea, it is not for you
This smoking body ploughs toward death.
It is not for the talkative blossoms of the sea
I drag my thin legs over the Chesapeake Bay,
Though perhaps by your motions the body heals.
For though on its road the body cannot march
With golden trumpets . . . it must march;
And the sea gives up its answer as it falls into itself.

DEFEATED

This burning behind my eyes as I open a door
Means that the blocky thing in my body has won.
The opaque sleep, heavy as October grass,
Grows stubbornly, triumphant even at midnight.

And another day disappears into the cliff.
Eskimos come to greet it with sharp cries.
Black water swells up over the new hole.
The ape, alone in his bamboo cage, smells

The python, and cries, but no one hears him call.
The grave moves forward from its ambush,
Curling slowly, with sideways motion,
Passing under bushes and through leaf tunnels,

Leaving dogs and sheep murdered where it slept.
Some shining thing inside us, that has
Served us well, shakes its bamboo bars.
It may be gone before we wake.

On a clear day, the jealous
Are jealous of ash leaves,
Flies, all jewelry of air.
They sit, gloating,
And grumpy with rage,
Under their blowing hair.

But the kind pine, though
Heavenless, does not drop
Green tears on earth.
And partnerships of sheep
Walk half asleep
On the mountains of death.

But a man may lose the jewel
On earth because
Of wife or job;
For what he saves
He cares nothing, and goes
Sullenly to a deep grave.

We are approaching sleep: the chestnut blossoms in the
    mind
Mingle with thoughts of pain
And the long roots of barley, bitterness
As of the oak roots staining the waters dark
In Louisiana, the wet streets soaked with rain
And sodden blossoms, out of this
We have come, a tunnel softly hurtling into darkness.

The storm is coming. The small farmhouse in Minnesota
Is hardly strong enough for the storm.
Darkness, darkness in grass, darkness in trees.
Even the water in wells trembles.
Bodies give off darkness, and chrysanthemums
Are dark, and horses, who are bearing great loads of hay
To the deep barns where the dark air is moving from
    corners.

Lincoln's statue, and the traffic. From the long past
Into the long present,
A bird, forgotten in these pressures, warbling,
As the great wheel turns around, grinding
The living in water.
Washing, continual washing, in water now stained
With blossoms and rotting logs,
Cries, half muffled, from beneath the earth, the living
    awakened at last like the dead.

Blessèd be the dancers! The dancers
Drumming the ground, the dancers
Driving the drums, shaking
Them out of their limbs!
And jumpers, leaping in darkness,
Dancing into space, invading
The last resorts of air, shaking
Nights out of the limbs,
And the dancers and jumpers and leapers!

I want the threshold to rise
Or lower, so that the drums
Beat along the green ground.
And I want the gate to open
Again, so that guards of the white stone
Stiffen in the morning air.
We want the Loosening One to come
At last, so that the leopards
Leap down from the light trees.

Dancers do not search for joy,
No more than the lion searches
For joy when he roves the night,
Nor for pain, no more than the ocean
Longs for pain when he roves the ground,
But for the green substance
In the lattices of the leaves,
In the high woods of the air,
In the wild holes of the sea.

GONE, GONE, GONE

"Search for the longing, O you who love me." OLD SAINT

When the wind-sleeve moves in the morning street,
I walk there, and brood on brown things,
On green things,
On the green waves
Lifting at sea, the green wives, and the brood of heaven.

I hear a faint sound, a bell inside the waves
Coming from far off . . . and the sweet clear
Bell of the joys
Of silence pierces
Through the roaring of cars, the hum of tires, the closing
    of doors.

When I hear that sound, a subtle force, a sheath,
Motherly, wraps me. Inside that sheath
I need no
House or land,
Caught in sweetness as the trout in the running stream.

Part Three

Poems mainly from
SILENCE IN
THE SNOWY FIELDS
and
THIS TREE WILL
BE HERE FOR
A THOUSAND YEARS

If we stay too long in solitude during our twenties, we are in danger. The old man who lives inside the young man may become a derelict, entirely cut off from community, family, sexual love, nature and spirit.

Yet at certain moments, particularly moments alone, we can pass into a deep of the mind, and at that instant we may pass as well into a tree or a hill, as when the dreamer traveling to some far place finds himself not farther from the soul but nearer to it, and wakes with the sweet sensation of friendship from other worlds. Whoever dreams in this way leaves judgment behind, at least temporarily, but we never leave mind. For when we pass into a deep of the mind, we become awake to the intelligence of hills and groves. At thirty-two I felt for the first time in adult life an unattached part of my soul join a tree standing in the center of a field. The tree's experience, existing without human companionship, and losing and gaining its leaves alone, was not unlike my own fragmentation, or estrangement, or unattachment. "The mind has shed leaves alone for years." When we pass into a deep of the mind, the soul follows its desire and attaches to ordinary earth, for the soul, as the old saying suggests, follows the path of water, and likes low places.

In such moments, prepared for by solitude and reading, I wrote a kind of poem I had never written before. It is not iambic, but free verse with distinct memories of form. Its shape is circular or spiral. The rhythm of the lines is sometimes weak, being adapted from Waley's translations of Chinese poems, Frank O'Connor's translations of Celtic poems, and my own translations of Machado, but a certain gaiety carries them along. The line breaks usually come where the thought ends, and bring a moment of silence. At the time I wrote: "If there is any poetry, it is in the white spaces between the stanzas."

I don't feel much human relationship in these poems, and the hundred thousand objects of twentieth-century life are absent also. I worked in the *Snowy Fields* poems to gain a resonance among the sounds, and hidden below that there is a second resonance between the soul and a loved countryside, in this case the countryside of my childhood. By that time, I had moved to a farm in western Minnesota near where I was born. I wrote a hundred or so of these poems during the three years from 1958 to 1961, there and during occasional stays in New York, and chose forty-four of them for *Silence in the Snowy Fields,* which became my first published book in 1962. I mostly stopped writing these poems in 1962, but a few still came every year, changed somewhat in form. A second group was published under the title *This Tree Will Be Here for a Thousand Years,* in 1979, and a third group will be published later.

AFTER DRINKING ALL NIGHT WITH A FRIEND, WE GO OUT IN A BOAT AT DAWN TO SEE WHO CAN WRITE THE BEST POEM

These pines, these fall oaks, these rocks,
This water dark and touched by wind—
I am like you, you dark boat,
Drifting over water fed by cool springs.

Beneath the waters, since I was a boy,
I have dreamt of strange and dark treasures,
Not of gold, or strange stones, but the true
Gift, beneath the pale lakes of Minnesota.

This morning also, drifting in the dawn wind,
I sense my hands, and my shoes, and this ink—
Drifting, as all of the body drifts,
Above the clouds of the flesh and the stone.

A few friendships, a few dawns, a few glimpses of grass,
A few oars weathered by the snow and the heat,
So we drift toward shore, over cold waters,
No longer caring if we drift or go straight.

I

What is so strange about a tree alone in an open field?
It is a willow tree. I walk around and around it.
The body is strangely torn, and cannot leave it.
At last I sit down beneath it.

II

It is a willow tree alone in acres of dry corn.
Its leaves are scattered around its trunk, and around me,
Brown now, and speckled with delicate black,
Only the cornstalks now can make a noise.

III

The sun is cold, burning through the frosty distances of
     space.
The weeds are frozen to death long ago.
Why then do I love to watch
The sun moving on the chill skin of the branches?

IV

The mind has shed leaves alone for years.
It stands apart with small creatures near its roots.
I am happy in this ancient place,
A spot easily caught sight of above the corn,
If I were a young animal ready to turn home at dusk.

The fall has come, clear as the eyes of chickens.
Awkward sounds come from the sea,
Sounds of muffled oarlocks
And swampings in lonely bays,
Surf crashing on unchristened shores,
And the wash of tiny snail shells in the wandering gravel.

My body also is lost or wandering: I know it,
As I cradle a pen, or walk down a stair
Holding a cup in my hand,
Not breaking into the pastures that lie in the sunlight.
This sloth is far inside the body,
The sloth of the body lost among the wandering stones of
     kindness.

Something homeless is looking on the long roads,
A dog lost since midnight, a box-elder
Bug who doesn't know
Its walls are gone, its house
Burnt. Even the young sun is lost,
Wandering over earth as the October night comes down.

SOLITUDE LATE AT NIGHT IN THE WOODS

I

The body is like a November birch facing the full moon
And reaching into the cold heavens.
In these trees there is no ambition, no sodden body, no
  leaves,
Nothing but bare trunks climbing like cold fire!

II

My last walk in the trees has come. At dawn
I must return to the trapped fields,
To the obedient earth.
The trees shall be reaching all the winter.

III

It is a joy to walk in the bare woods.
The moonlight is not broken by the heavy leaves.
The leaves are down, and touching the soaked earth,
Giving off the odor that partridges love.

I

The grass is half-covered with snow.
It was the sort of snowfall that starts in late afternoon,
And now the little houses of the grass are growing dark.

II

If I reached my hands down, near the earth,
I could take handfuls of darkness!
A darkness was always there, which we never noticed.

III

As the snow grows heavier, the cornstalks fade farther
    away,
And the barn moves nearer to the house.
The barn moves all alone in the growing storm.

IV

The barn is full of corn, and moving toward us now,
Like a hulk blown toward us in a storm at sea;
All the sailors on deck have been blind for many years.

The dark geese treading blowing Dakota snows
Over the fence stairs of the small farms come,
Slipping through cries flung up into the night,
And settling, ah, between them, shifting wings,
Light down at last in bare and snowy fields.

The drunken father has pulled the boy inside.
The boy breaks free, turns, leaves the house.
He spends that night out eating with the geese
Where, alert and balancing on wide feet,
Crossing rows, they walk through the broken stalks.

How strange to think of giving up all ambition!
Suddenly I see with such clear eyes
The white flake of snow
That has just fallen on the horse's mane!

THREE KINDS OF PLEASURES

I

Sometimes, riding in a car, in Wisconsin
Or Illinois, you notice those dark telephone poles
One by one lift themselves out of the fence line
And slowly leap on the gray sky—
And past them the snowy fields.

II

The darkness drifts down like snow on the picked
    cornfields
In Wisconsin, and on these black trees
Scattered, one by one,
Through the winter fields—
We see stiff weeds and brownish stubble,
And white snow left now only in the wheeltracks of the
    combine.

III

It is a pleasure, also, to be driving
Toward Chicago, near dark,
And see the lights in the barns.
The bare trees more dignified than ever,
Like a fierce man on his deathbed,
And the ditches along the road half full of a private
    snow.

I start out for a walk at last after weeks at the desk.
Moon gone, plowing underfoot, no stars; not a trace of
    light!
Suppose a horse were galloping toward me in this open
    field?
Every day I did not spend in solitude was wasted.

AFTER WORKING

After many strange thoughts, thoughts
Of distant harbors and new life,
I came in and found the moonlight lying in the room.

Outside it covers the trees like pure sound,
The sound of tower bells, or water moving under the ice;
The sound of the deaf hearing through the bones of their
     heads.

We know the road. As the moonlight
Lifts everything, so in a night like this
The road goes on ahead. . . . It is all clear.

EARLY SPRING BETWEEN MADISON AND BELLINGHAM

When our privacy starts over again,
How beautiful the things are we did not notice before!
A few sweetclover plants that blossom yellow
Along the road to Bellingham,
A culvert end that pokes out of a driveway . . .
The wooden corncrib that slowly collapses.
What no one loves, no one rushes toward, or shouts
    about,
What lives like the new moon,
And the wind
Blowing against the rumps of grazing cows.

Telephone wires stretching across water,
The drowned sailor appears at the foot of his mother's
    bed,
The grandfather and grandson sitting together.

I get up late and ask what has to be done today.
Nothing has to be done, so the farm looks doubly good.
The blowing maple leaves fit so well with the moving
    grass.
The shadow of my writing shack looks small beside the
    growing trees.

Never be with your children, let them get skinny like
    radishes!
Let your wife worry about the lack of money!
Your whole life is like some drunkard's dream.
You haven't combed your hair for a whole month.

OLD BOARDS

I

I love to see boards lying on the ground in early spring:
The ground beneath them is wet and muddy—
Perhaps covered with chicken tracks—
And they are dry and eternal.

II

This is the wood one sees on the decks of ocean ships,
Wood that carries us far from land,
With a dryness of something used for simple tasks,
Like a horse's tail.

III

This wood is like a man who has a simple life,
Living through the spring and winter on the ship of his
    own desire.
He sits on dry wood surrounded by half-melted snow
As the rooster walks away springily over the dampened
    hay.

There is unknown dust that is near us,
Waves breaking on shores just over the hill,
Trees full of birds that we have never seen,
Nets drawn down with dark fish.

The evening arrives; we look up and it is there.
It has come through the nets of the stars,
Through the tissues of the grass,
Walking quietly over the asylums of the water.

The day shall never end, we think;
We have hair that seems born for the daylight.
But, at last, the quiet waters of the night will rise,
And our skin shall see far off, as it does under water.

I

Oh, on an early morning I think I shall live forever!
I am wrapped in my joyful flesh,
As the grass is wrapped in its clouds of green.

II

Rising from a bed, where I dreamt
Of long rides past castles, and hot coals,
The sun lies happily on my knees;
I have suffered and survived the night
Bathed in dark water, like any blade of grass.

III

The strong leaves of the box elder tree,
Plunging in the wind, call us to disappear
Into the wilds of the universe,
Where we shall sit at the foot of a plant,
And live forever, like the dust.

The day is awake. The bark calls to the rain still in the
    cloud:
"Never forget the lonely taste of the white dew."
And woolen-robed drummers call on the naked to dance;
All the particles of the body shout together.

Sitting on the disc, the morning dove coos a porch, then a
    cathedral,
Then the two arms of the cross!

He gives the nose, then the head, then the two ears of
    this rabbit
Hopping along the garden,
Then his death. . . .

After that we will be alone in the deep blue reaches of
    the river.

Inside the veins there are navies setting forth,
Tiny explosions at the waterlines,
And seagulls weaving in the wind of the salty blood.

It is the morning. The country has slept the whole
winter.
Window seats were covered with fur skins, the yard was
full
Of stiff dogs, and hands that clumsily held heavy books.

Now we wake, and rise from bed, and eat breakfast!
Shouts rise from the harbor of the blood,
Mist, and masts rising, the knock of wooden tackle in the
sunlight.

Now we sing, and do tiny dances on the kitchen floor.
Our whole body is like a harbor at dawn;
We know that our master has left us for the day.

DRIVING TOWARD THE
LAC QUI PARLE RIVER

I

I am driving; it is dusk; Minnesota.
The stubble field catches the last growth of sun.
The soybeans are breathing on all sides.
Old men are sitting before their houses on car seats
In the small towns. I am happy,
The moon rising above the turkey sheds.

II

The small world of the car
Plunges through the deep fields of the night,
On the road from Willmar to Milan.
This solitude covered with iron
Moves through the fields of night
Penetrated by the noise of crickets.

III

Nearly to Milan, suddenly a small bridge,
And water kneeling in the moonlight.
In small towns the houses are built right on the ground;
The lamplight falls on all fours on the grass.
When I reach the river, the full moon covers it.
A few people are talking, low, in a boat.

From far out in the center of the naked lake
The loon's cry rose.
It was the cry of someone who owned very little.

NIGHT

I

If I think of a horse wandering about sleeplessly
All night on this short grass covered with moonlight,
I feel a joy, as if I had thought
Of a pirate ship ploughing through dark flowers.

II

The box elders around us are full of joy,
Obeying what is beneath them.
The lilacs are sleeping, and the plants are sleeping;
Even the wood made into a casket is asleep.

III

The butterfly is carrying loam on his wings;
The toad is bearing tiny bits of granite in his skin.
The leaves at the crown of the tree are asleep
Like the dark bits of earth at its root.

IV

Alive, we are like a sleek black water beetle.
Skating across still water in any direction
We choose, and soon to be swallowed
Suddenly from beneath.

Empty places are white and light-footed. "Taking the road" means being willing to die, like the pigeon grass clump that dies so quietly. There is a joy in emptiness. One day I saw an empty corncob on the ground, so beautiful, and where each kernel had been, there was a place to live.

The eyes are drawn to the dusty ground in fall—
pieces of crushed oyster shell
like doors into the earth made of mother-of-pearl,
slivers of glass,
a white chicken's feather that still seems excited by the
    warm blood,
and a corncob, all kernels gone, room after room in its
    endless palace . . .
this is the palace, the place of many mansions,
which Christ has gone to prepare for us.

READING IN FALL RAIN

The fields are black once more.
The old restlessness is going.
I reach out with open arms
to pull in the black fields.

All morning rain has fallen
steadily on the roof.
I feel like a butterfly
joyful in its powerful cocoon.

*　*　*

I break off reading:
one of my bodies is gone!
It's outdoors, walking
swiftly away in the rain!

I get up and look out.
Sure enough, I see
the rooster lifting his legs
high in the wet grass.

CORNPICKER POEM

I

Sheds left out in the darkness,
Abandoned granaries, cats merging into the night.

There are hubcaps cooling in the dark yard.

The stiff-haired son has slouched in
And gone to bed.
A low wind sweeps over the moony land.

II

Overshoes stiffen in the entry.
The calendar grows rigid on the wall.

He dreams, and his body grows limber.
He is fighting a many-armed woman;
He is a struggler, he will not yield.
He fights her in the crotch of a willow tree.

He wakes up with jaws set,
And a victory.

III

It is dawn. Cornpicking today.
He leans over, hurtling
His old Pontiac down the road.

Somewhere the sullen chilled machine
Is waiting, its empty gas cans around it.

That afternoon I had been fishing alone,
Strong wind, some water slopping in the back of the boat.
I was far from home.
Later I woke several times hearing geese.
I dreamt I saw retarded children playing, and one came
    near,
And her teacher, face open, hair light.
For the first time I forgot my distance;
I took her in my arms and held her.

Waking up, I felt how alone I was.
I walked on the dock,
Fishing alone in the far north.

DIGGING WORMS

Here I am, digging worms behind the chickenhouse,
The clods fall open when I hit
Them with a tine, worms fall out. . . .

Dreams press us on all sides, we stagger
Along a wire, our children balance us
On their shoulders, we balance their graves
On ours.

Their graves are light. And we unwind
From some kind of cocoon made by lovers. . . .
The old tires we used to swing on,
Going faster, around and around, until

With one lurch we grow still and look down at our
    shoes.
Last night I dreamt my carelessness started stones
    dislodging near a castle. The stones
Did not hurt my shoulders when they hit and went
    through,
But the wall of the castle fell.

LATE MOON

The third-week moon reaches its light over my father's
    farm,
Half of it dark now, in the west that eats it away.
The earth has rocks in it that hum at early dawn.
As I turn to go in, I see my shadow reach for the latch.

I woke from a first-day-of-snow dream.
I met a girl in the attic,
    who talked of operas, intensely.
Snow has bent the poplar over nearly to the ground;
New snowfall widens the plowing.
Outside, maple leaves float on rainwater,
    yellow, matted, luminous.
I saw a salamander . . . I took him up . . .
He was cold. When I put him down again,
    he strode over a log
With such confidence, like a chessmaster,
    the front leg first, then the hind
    leg, he rose up like a tractor climbing
    over a hump in the field
And disappeared toward winter, a caravan going deeper
    into mountains,
Dogs pulling travois,
Feathers fluttering on the lances of the arrogant men.

Night of first snow.
I stand, my back against a board fence.
The fir tree is black at the trunk, white out at the edges.
The earth balances all around my feet.

The trunk joins the white ground with what is above.
Fir branches balance the snow.
I too am a dark shape vertical to the earth.
All over the sky, the gray color that pleases the snow
      mother.

Between boards I see three hairs a rabbit left behind
As he scooted under the fence.
A woman walks out toward the wicker basket
Rocking in darkening reeds.
The Bride is inside the basket where Moses sleeps.
What is human lies in the way the basket is rocking.

I

About four, a few flakes.
I empty the teapot out in the snow,
Feeling shoots of joy in the new cold.
By nightfall, wind,
The curtains on the south sway softly.

II

My shack has two rooms; I use one.
The lamplight falls on my chair and table,
And I fly into one of my own poems—
I can't tell you where—
As if I appeared where I am now,
In a wet field, snow falling.

III

More of the fathers are dying each day.
It is time for the sons.
Bits of darkness are gathering around them.
The darkness appears as flakes of light.

IV On Meditation

There is a solitude like black mud!
Sitting in this darkness singing,
I can't tell if this joy
Is from the body, or the soul, or a third place!

V *Listening to Bach*
Inside this music there is someone
Who is not well described by the names
Of Jesus, or Jehovah, or the Lord of Hosts!

VI
When I woke, a new snow had fallen.
I am alone, yet someone else is with me,
Drinking coffee, looking out at the snow.

It is late December; I walk through the pasture.
Light on the hillocks, light
On the rolling mounds, eaten clean by horse teeth.

Then the black plowing—clods turned up.
The shoe looks for solid home.
A half-covered ear of corn
Not found by a deer.

I am learning; I walk through the plowed fields,
With a bag, picking up corn for the horses.
Some small pebbles on the dirt road
On the way home alight in the late sun.
Surely we do not eat only with our mouths,
Or drink only by lifting our hands!

Who is this out gathering moss by the seashore?
"My master has gone picking ferns on the mountain."
No one knows what they were picking.
What they drink is something respectable people do not
    want to take in,
Walking in fog near the cliff.

AN EVENING WHEN THE FULL MOON ROSE AS THE SUN SET

April 11, 1976

The sun goes down in the dusty April night.
"You know it could be alive!"
The sun is round, massive, compelling, sober, on fire.
It moves swiftly through the tree stalks of the Lundin
    grove as we drive past. . . .
The legs of a bronze god walking at the edge of the world,
    unseen by many,
On his archaic errands, doubled up on his own energy.
He guides his life by his dreams;
When we look again he is gone.

Turning toward Milan, we see the other one, the moon,
    whole and rising.
Three wild geese make dark spots in that part of the sky.
Under the shining one the pastures leap forward,
Grass fields rolling as in October, the sow-colored fields
    near the river.
This rising one lights the pair of pintails alert in the
    shallow pond.
It shines on those faithful to each other, alert in the early
    night.
And the life of faithfulness goes by like a river,
With no one noticing it.

Part Four

Poems on the Vietnam War from
THE LIGHT AROUND
THE BODY (1967)

and

THE TEETH MOTHER
NAKED AT LAST (1970)

The Vietnam War and the revulsion against it came down like a rainstorm and carried us away. The first strong protests came in 1965. I had been composing for the previous six or seven years a book called *Poems for the Ascension of J. P. Morgan,* in which, encouraged by Neruda's poetry, I wrote of historical figures. Unlike *Silence in the Snowy Fields,* it was a book of judgment rather than of affinity, and the poems on the Vietnam War were a continuation of that series. The three poems "The Executive's Death," "Pilgrim Fish Heads," and "Romans Angry at the Inner World" belong to that series, and I'll place them here as an introduction to the war poems.

The many hours I spent translating Neruda, Vallejo, Antonio Machado, Aleixandre, and Lorca brought me into a community of poets, who believed that it was just and natural to write of important national griefs in one's poetry as well as of private griefs. Encouraged by that community, I began the robber baron poems in a mood of privacy, but the Vietnam War changed the way I lived: the psychic urgency dissolved calmness for most of us, and actively opposing the war meant an end to long periods of solitude.

Reciting political poems at Vietnam gatherings, I experienced for the first time in my life the power of spoken or oral poetry. A briefly lasting community springs to life in front of the voice, like a flower opening—it can be a community either of excitement or of feeling. The community flowers when the poem is spoken in the ancient way—that is, with full sound, with conviction, and with the knowledge that the emotions are not private to the person speaking them.

The inner and spiral form of *Snowy Fields* poems was not appropriate for poetry about political power, and I decided for *The Teeth Mother Naked at Last* on a line that embodies power in a direct way. I wrote in a line adapted from earlier poets that throws or catapults itself into the outer world, and composed a number of passages while reciting. I've set down a discussion of this line for those interested in an essay at the back of this book.

After its years of storm, the war ended in 1975. The war had eroded the confidence of men in each other, especially the confidence of younger men in older men, and it emphasized how estranged from nature the entire nation was. It was as if the hostile mountain spirit had defeated the entire nation. The war brought a new corruption of language. The practice of doing ugly things, then describing them in bland words, which Hawthorne wrote of in "Young Goodman Brown," thinking of it as a habit of Christian commercial people, became national policy. Since the leaders admitted to no shadow, the opposition called them all shadow, and the exaggerations on both sides damaged the language of public debate in the United States. By the end of the war, I felt some affinity gone in me, and I wanted to return to privacy rather than to go on judging, useful as judgment is.

THE EXECUTIVE'S DEATH

Merchants have multiplied more than the stars of heaven.
Half the population are like the long grasshoppers
That sleep in the bushes in the cool of the day;
The sound of their wings is heard at noon, muffled, near
    the earth.
The crane handler dies; the taxi driver dies, slumped over
In his taxi. Meanwhile high in the air an executive
Walks on cool floors, and suddenly falls.
Dying, he dreams he is lost in a snowbound mountain
On which he crashed, carried at night by great machines.
As he lies on the wintry slope, cut off and dying,
A pine stump talks to him of Goethe and Jesus.
Commuters arrive in Hartford at dusk like moles
Or hares flying from a fire behind them,
And the dusk in Hartford is full of their sighs.
Their trains come through the air like a dark music,
Like the sound of horns, the sound of thousands of small
    wings.

What shall the world do with its children?
There are lives the executives
Know nothing of:
A leaping of the body,
The body rolling—I have felt it—
And we float
Joyfully toward the dark places.
But the executioners
Move toward Drusia. They tie her legs
On the iron horse. "Here is a woman
Who has seen our Mother
In the other world." Next they warm
The hooks. The two Romans had put their trust
In the outer world. Irons glowed
Like teeth. They wanted her
To assure them. She refused. Finally
They took burning
Pine sticks, and pushed them
Into her sides. Her breath rose
And she died. The executioners
Rolled her off onto the ground.
A light snow began to fall from the clear sky
And covered the mangled body.
And the executives, astonished, withdrew.
The inner world is a thorn
In the ear of a tiny beast!
The fingers of the executive are too thick
To pull it out.
It is a jagged stone
Flying toward us out of the darkness.

It is a Pilgrim village; heavy rain is falling.
Fish heads lie smiling at the corners of houses.
Inside, words like "Samson" hang from the rafters.
Outdoors, the chickens squawk in woody hovels,
yet the chickens are walking on Calvinist ground.
The women move through the dark kitchen; their heavy
skirts bear them down like drowning men.
Upstairs, beds are like thunderstorms on the bare floor,
leaving the covers always moist by the rough woods.
And the eggs! Strange, white, perfect eggs!
Eggs that even the rain could not move,
white, painless, with tails even in nightmares.
And the Indian, damp, musky, asking for a bed.
The Mattapoiset is in league with rotting wood;
he has made a conspiracy with the salamander;
he has made treaties with the cold heads of fishes.
In the grave he does not rot, but vanishes into water.
The Indian goes on living in the rain-soaked stumps.
This is our enemy; this is the outcast;
the one from whom we must protect our nation,
the one whose dark hair hides us from the sun.

AT A MARCH AGAINST THE VIETNAM WAR

Washington, November 27, 1965

Newspapers rise high in the air over Maryland.

We walk about, bundled in coats and sweaters in the late
    November sun.
Looking down, I see feet moving
Calmly, gaily,
Almost as if separated from their bodies.

But there is something moving in the dark somewhere
Just beyond
The edge of our eyes: a boat
Covered with machine guns
Moving along under trees.

It is black.
The hand reaches out
But cannot touch it. . . .
It is that darkness among pine boughs
That the Puritans brushed
As they went out to kill turkeys.

At the edge of the jungle clearing
It explodes
On the ground.

We have carried around this cup of darkness.
We hesitate to anoint ourselves.
Now we pour it over our heads.

ASIAN PEACE OFFERS REJECTED
WITHOUT PUBLICATION

These suggestions by Asians are not taken seriously.
We know Rusk smiles as he passes them to someone.
Men like Rusk are not men only—
They are bombs waiting to be loaded in a darkened
    hangar.
Rusk's assistants eat hurriedly,
Talking of Teilhard de Chardin,
Longing to get back to their offices
So they can cling to the underside of the steel wings
    shuddering faintly in the high altitudes.
They disembark first, and hand the coffee cup to the
    drawn pilot.
They start the projector, and show the movie about the
    mad professor.

Lost angels huddled on a night branch!
The waves crossing
And recrossing beneath—
The sound of the rampaging Missouri—
Bending the reeds again and again—something inside us
Like a ghost train in the Rockies
About to be buried in snow!
Its long hoot
Making the owl in the Douglas fir turn his head . . .

JOHNSON'S CABINET WATCHED BY ANTS

I

It is a clearing deep in a forest: overhanging boughs
Make a low place. Here the citizens we know during the
    day,
The ministers, the department heads,
Appear changed: the stockholders of large steel companies
In small wooden shoes; here are the generals dressed as
    gamboling lambs.

II

Tonight they burn the rice supplies; tomorrow
They lecture on Thoreau; tonight they move around the
    trees;
Tomorrow they pick the twigs from their clothes;
Tonight they throw the firebombs; tomorrow
They read the Declaration of Independence; tomorrow
    they are in church.

III

Ants are gathered around an old tree.
In a choir they sing, in harsh and gravelly voices,
Old Etruscan songs on tyranny.
Toads nearby clap their small hands, and join
The fiery songs, their five long toes trembling in the
    soaked earth.

One night we find ourselves near the giant's house.
At dawn mist blows over the great meadow.
Outside the steps we find an aunt and uncle
Dead for twenty years working with hoes.
In flower beds small old men are growing from the
    ground.
A mill grinding. We go in. Chairs
In the great room, hacked from redwood.
Tiny loaves of bread with ears lie on the President's
    table.
Steps coming! The father will soon return!

There are longings to kill that cannot be seen,
Or are seen only by a minister who no longer believes in
   God,
Living in his parish like a crow in its nest.

And there are flowers with murky centers,
Impenetrable, ebony, basalt.

Conestogas go past, over the Platte, murderers
From the Carolinas riding under the canvas.

Who are our enemies? Perhaps the soldiers
And the poor, those "unable to rejoice."

The bombers spread out, temperature steady.
A Negro's ear sleeping in an automobile tire.
Pieces of timber float by, saying nothing.

*   *   *

Bishops rush about crying, "There is no war,"
And bombs fall,
Leaving a dust on the beech trees.

*   *   *

One leg walks down the road and leaves
The other behind; the eyes part
And fly off in opposite directions.

*   *   *

Filaments of death grow out.
The sheriff cuts off his black legs
And nails them to a tree.

COUNTING SMALL-BONED BODIES

Let's count the bodies over again.

If we could only make the bodies smaller,
the size of skulls,
we could make a whole plain white with skulls in the
    moonlight.

If we could only make the bodies smaller,
maybe we could fit
a whole year's kill in front of us on a desk.

If we could only make the bodies smaller,
we could fit
a body into a finger ring, for a keepsake forever.

DRIVING THROUGH MINNESOTA DURING
THE HANOI BOMBINGS

We drive between lakes just turning green;
Late June. The white turkeys have been moved
A second time to new grass.
How long the seconds are in great pain!
Terror just before death,
Shoulders torn, shot
From helicopters. "I saw the boy
being tortured with a telephone generator,"
The sergeant said.
"I felt sorry for him
And blew his head off with a shotgun."
These instants become crystals,
Particles
The grass cannot dissolve. Our own gaiety
Will end up
In Asia, and you will look down in your cup
And see
Black Starfighters.
Our own cities were the ones we wanted to bomb!
Therefore we will have to
Go far away
To atone
For the suffering of the stringy-chested
And the short rice-fed ones, quivering
In the helicopter like wild animals,
Shot in the chest, taken back to be questioned.

I hear spokesmen praising Tsombe, and the Portuguese
In Angola. These are the men who skinned Little Crow!
We are all their sons, skulking
In back rooms, selling nails with trembling hands!

We fear every person on earth with black hair.
We send teams to overthrow Chief Joseph's government.
We train natives to kill the President with blowdarts.
We have men loosening the nails on Noah's ark.

State Department men float in the heavy jellies near the
    bottom
Like exhausted crustaceans, like squids who are confused,
Sending out beams of black light to the open sea.
Each fights his fraternal feeling for the great landlords.

We have violet rays that light up the jungle at night,
    showing us
The friendly populations; and we teach the children of
    ritual,
The forest children, to overcome their longing for life,
    and we send
Sparks of black light that fit the holes in the generals'
    eyes.

Underneath all the cement of the Pentagon
There is a drop of Indian blood preserved in snow:
Preserved from a trail of blood that once led away
From the stockade, over the snow, the trail now lost.

THE TEETH MOTHER NAKED AT LAST

I

Massive engines lift beautifully from the deck.
Wings appear over the trees, wings with eight hundred
    rivets.

Engines burning a thousand gallons of gasoline a minute
    sweep over the huts with dirt floors.
Chickens feel the fear deep in the pits of their beaks.
Buddha and Padma Sambhava.

Meanwhile out on the China Sea
immense gray bodies are floating,
born in Roanoke,
the ocean to both sides expanding, "buoyed on the dense
    marine."

Helicopters flutter overhead. The death-
bee is coming. Super Sabres
like knots of neurotic energy sweep
around and return.
This is Hamilton's triumph.
This is the triumph of a centralized bank.
B-52s come from Guam. Teachers
die in flames. The hopes of Tolstoy fall asleep in the ant
    heap.
Do not ask for mercy.

Now the time comes to look into the past-tunnels,
hours given and taken in school,
the scuffles in coatrooms,
foam leaps from his nostrils.

Now we come to the scum one takes from the mouths of
the dead.
Now we sit beside the dying, and hold their hands, there
is hardly time for goodbye.
The staff sergeant from North Carolina is dying—you
hold his hand.
He knows the mansions of the dead are empty.
He has an empty place inside him,
created one night when his parents came home drunk.
He uses half his skin to cover it,
as you try to protect a balloon from sharp objects.

Artillery shells explode. Napalm canisters roll end over
end.
Eight hundred steel pellets fly through the vegetable
walls.
The six-hour-old infant puts his fists instinctively to his
eyes to keep out the light.
But the room explodes.
The children explode.
Blood leaps on the vegetable walls.

Yes, I know, blood leaps on the vegetable walls. . . .
Don't cry at that.
Do you cry at the wind pouring out of Canada?
Do you cry for the reeds shaken at the edge of the marsh?
The Marine battalion enters.
This happens when the seasons change.
This happens when the leaves begin to drop from the
trees too early.
"Kill them: I don't want to see anything moving."

This happens when the ice begins to show its teeth in the
 ponds.
This happens when the heavy layers of lake water press
 down on the fish's head,
and send him deeper, where his tail swirls slowly,
and his brain passes him pictures of heavy reeds, of
 vegetation fallen on vegetation. . . .
Now the Marine knives sweep around like sharp-edged
 jets;
they slice open the rice bags, the reed walls, the
 mattresses.
Marines kill ducks with three-hundred-dollar shotguns
and lift cigarette lighters to light the thatched roofs of
 huts.
They watch the old women warily.

        II
Excellent Roman knives slip along the ribs.
A stronger man starts to jerk up the strips of flesh.
"Let's hear it again: you believe in the Father, and the
 Son, and the Holy Ghost?"
A long scream unrolls.
More.
*"From the political point of view, democratic institutions
 are being built in Vietnam, wouldn't you agree?"*

A green parrot shudders under the fingernails.
Blood jumps in the pocket.
The scream lashes like a tail.

*"Let us not be de-terred from our task by the voices of
     dis-sent. . . ."*
The whines of the jets
pierce like a long needle.

As soon as the President finishes his press conference,
     black wings carry off the words,
bits of flesh still clinging to them.

*   *   *

The ministers lie, the professors lie, the television
     reporters lie, the priests lie.
What are these lies? They mean that the country wants
     to die.
Lie after lie starts out into the prairie grass,
like mile-long caravans of Conestoga wagons crossing the
     Platte.

And a long desire for death goes with them, guiding it all
     from beneath:
"a death longing if all longing else be vain,"
stringing together the vague and foolish words.

It is a desire to eat death,
to gobble it down,
to rush on it like a cobra with mouth open.
It is a desire to take death inside,
to feel it burning inside, pushing out velvety hairs,
like a clothesbrush in the intestines—

That is the thrill that leads the President on to lie.

Now the Chief Executive enters, and the press
    conference begins.
First the President lies about the date the Appalachian
    Mountains rose.
Then he lies about the population of Chicago,
then the weight of the adult eagle, and the acreage of the
    Everglades.
Next he lies about the number of fish taken every year in
    the Arctic.

He has private information about which city *is* the capital
    of Wyoming.
He lies next about the birthplace of Attila the Hun,
Then about the composition of the amniotic fluid.

He insists that Luther was never a German,
and only the Protestants sold indulgences.
He declares that Pope Leo X *wanted* to reform the
    Church, but the liberal elements prevented him.
He declares the Peasants' War was fomented by Italians
    from the North.
And the Attorney General lies about the time the sun
    sets.

* * *

These lies mean that something in the nation wants to
    die.

What is there now to hold us to earth? We long to go.
It is the longing for someone to come and take us by the
hand to where they all are sleeping:
where the Egyptian pharaohs are asleep, and our own
mothers,
and all those disappeared children, who went around
with us on the rings at grade school.

Do not be angry at the President—
He is longing to take in his hands the locks of death-hair:
to meet his own children, dead, or never born. . . .

He is drifting sideways toward the dusty places.

III
This is what it's like for a rich country to make war.
This is what it's like to bomb huts (afterwards described
as "structures").
This is what it's like to kill marginal farmers (afterwards
described as "Communists").

This is what it's like to see the altimeter needle going
mad:

*Baron 25, this is 81. Are there any friendlies in the area?
81 from 25, negative on the friendlies. I'd like you to
take out as many structures as possible located in those
trees within 200 meters east and west of my smoke mark.*

diving, the green earth swinging, cheeks hanging back,
red pins blossoming ahead of us, 20-millimeter cannon

fire, leveling off, ricefields shooting by like telephone
poles, smoke rising, hut roofs loom up huge as landing
fields, slugs going in, half the huts on fire, small figures
running, palm trees burning, shooting past, up again
. . . blue sky . . . cloud mountains . . .

This is what it's like to have a gross national product.

This is what it's like to send firebombs down from air-
    conditioned cockpits.
This is what it's like to fire into a reed hut with an
    automatic weapon.

When St. Francis renounced his father's goods,
when he threw his clothes on the court floor,
then the ability to kiss the poor leapt up from the floor to
    his lips.
We claim our father's clothes, and pick up other people's;
finally we have three or four layers of clothes.
Then all at once it is fated, we cannot help ourselves,
we fire into a reed hut with an automatic weapon.

It's because the aluminum window-shade business is
    doing so well in the United States
that we spread fire over entire villages.
It's because the trains coming into New Jersey hit the
    right switches every day
that Vietnamese men are cut in two by bullets that
    follow each other like freight trains.

It's because the average hospital bed now costs two
    hundred dollars a day
that we bomb the hospitals in the north.

It is because we have so few women sobbing in back
    rooms,
because we have so few children's heads torn apart by
    high-velocity bullets,
because we have so few tears falling on our own hands,
that the Super Sabre turns and screams down toward the
    earth.

IV
A car is rolling toward a rock wall.
The treads in the face begin to crack.
We all feel like tires being run down roads under heavy
    cars.

The teen-ager imagines herself floating through the Seven
    Spheres.
Oven doors are found
open.
Soot collects over the doorframe, has children, takes
    courses, goes mad, and dies.

There is a black silo inside our bodies, revolving fast.
Bits of black paint are flaking off,
where the motorcycles roar, around and around,
rising higher on the silo walls,
the bodies bent toward the horizon,
driven by angry women dressed in black.

I know that books are tired of us.
I *know* they are chaining the Bible to chairs.
Books don't want to remain in the same room with us
    anymore.
New Testaments are escaping . . . dressed as women . . .
    they slip out after dark.
And Plato! Plato . . . Plato
wants to hurry back up the river of time,
so he can end as a blob of seaflesh rotting on an
    Australian beach.

V

Why are they dying? I have written this so many times.
They are dying because the President has opened a Bible
    again.
They are dying because gold deposits have been found
    among the Shoshoni Indians.
They are dying because money follows intellect,
and intellect is like a fan opening in the wind.

The Marines think that unless they die the rivers will not
    move.
They are dying so that the mountain shadows will
    continue to fall east in the afternoon,
so that the beetle can move along the ground near the
    fallen twigs.

VI

But if one of those children came near that we have set
    on fire,

came toward you like a gray barn, walking,
you would howl like a wind tunnel in a hurricane,
you would tear at your shirt with blue hands,
you would drive over your own child's wagon trying to
    back up,
the pupils of your eyes would go wild.

If a child came by burning, you would dance on your
    lawn,
trying to leap into the air, digging into your cheeks,
you would ram your head against the wall of your
    bedroom
like a bull penned too long in his moody pen.

If one of those children came toward me with both hands
in the air, fire rising along both elbows,
I would suddenly go back to my animal brain,
I would drop on all fours screaming;
my vocal cords would turn blue; so would yours.
It would be two days before I could play with one of my
    own children again.

VII
I want to sleep awhile in the rays of the sun slanting over
    the snow.
Don't wake me.
Don't tell me how much grief there is in the leaf with its
    natural oils.
Don't tell me how many children have been born with
    stumpy hands
all those years we lived in St. Augustine's shadow.

Tell me about the dust that falls from the yellow daffodil
    shaken in the restless winds.
Tell me about the particles of Babylonian thought that
    still pass through the earthworm every day.
Don't tell me about "the frightening laborers who do not
    read books."

The mad beast covered with European hair rushes
    towards the mesa bushes in Mendocino County.
Pigs rush toward the cliff.
The waters underneath part: in one ocean luminous
    globes float up (in them hairy and ecstatic men);
in the other the Teeth Mother, naked at last.

Let us drive cars
up
the light beams
to the stars. . . .

And return to earth
and live inside the drop of sweat
that falls from the chin of the Protestant tied in the fire.

Part Five

Prose Poems mostly from

THE MORNING GLORY (1975)

All poems are journeys. They go from somewhere to somewhere else. The best poems take long journeys. I like poetry best that journeys—while remaining in the human scale—to the other world, which may be a place as easily overlooked as a bee's wing.

Some poems carry us on their sound, and other poems carry us to the new place on their minute detail, on what they give us to see. If we write of dreams and feelings only, we can find ourselves trapped in mine shafts for years, wandering, longing for the light.

When I try to embody in language what the eyes see, I like the mildly hypnotic rhythms of prose. Does poetry wake us up or put us to sleep? Yeats had no doubt; the function of meter, he said, is to put us into a trance, so that we can approach one of the far places of the mind; and the poet accordingly chooses the particular rhythm appropriate to the trance he wishes for the reader and for himself. A poet writing prose poems, then, is not more respectful than the metered poet of the reader's privacy or mindfulness; he puts you into a different sort of trance. All good poetry, including prose poetry, acts to shut off the part of the brain that is always ready to be alarmed, convulsively curling around itself, and acts to open up the part of the brain that takes in a more relaxed breathing. The difference between lulling prose and the good prose poem is that the urgent, alert rhythm of the prose poem prepares us to journey, to cross the border, either to the other world, or to that place where the animal lives. I wrote the first poem of this sort when Mary at three brought me an English caterpillar. Since then I've written prose poems about a hollow tree, a bouquet of roses, a starfish, a dried sturgeon, and many other objects. The one who writes seeing poems, then, is not the dreamer or the judge, but the giver of attention. The old people say that each object in the universe—seashell, bat's wing, pine cone, patch of lichen—contains some fragment of our missing soul, and so our soul is thin. Making journeys of this sort could be called thickening the soul.

Alone on the jagged rock at the south end of Mc-
Clure's Beach. The sky low. The sea grows more and more
private, as afternoon goes on; the sky comes down closer;
the unobserved water rushes out to the horizon, horses
galloping in a mountain valley at night. The waves smash
up the rock; I find flags of seaweed high on the worn top,
forty feet up, thrown up overnight; separated water still
pooled there, like the black ducks that fly desolate, forlorn,
and joyful over the seething swells, who never "feel pity
for themselves," and "do not lie awake weeping for their
sins." In their blood cells the vultures coast with furry
necks extended, watching over the desert for signs of life
to end. It is not our life we need to weep for. Inside us
there is some secret. We are following a narrow ledge
around a mountain, we are sailing on skeletal eerie craft
over the buoyant ocean.

I bend over an old hollow cottonwood stump, still standing, waist high, and look inside. Early spring. Its Siamese temple walls are all brown and ancient. The walls have been worked on by the intricate ones. Inside the hollow walls there is privacy and secrecy, dim light. And yet some creature has died here.

On the temple floor feathers, gray feathers, many of them with a fluted whitetip. Many feathers. In the silence many feathers.

It is low tide. Fog. I have climbed down the cliffs from Pierce Ranch to the tide pools. Now the ecstasy of the low tide, kneeling down, alone. In six inches of clear water I notice a purple starfish—with nineteen arms! It is a delicate purple, the color of old carbon paper, or an attic dress . . . at the webs between the arms sometimes a more intense sunset red glows through. The fingers are relaxed . . . some curled up at the tips . . . with delicate rods . . . apparently globes on top of each, as at world's fairs, waving about. The starfish slowly moves up the groin of the rock . . . then back down . . . many of its arms rolled up now, lazily, like a puppy on its back. One arm is especially active and curves up over its own body as if a dinosaur were looking behind him.

How slowly and evenly it moves! The starfish is a glacier, going sixty miles a year! It moves over the pink rock, by means I cannot see . . . and into marvelously floating delicate brown weeds. It is about the size of the bottom of a pail. When I reach out to it, it tightens and then slowly relaxes. . . . I take an arm and quickly lift. The underside is a pale tan. . . . Gradually, as I watch, thousands of tiny tubes begin rising from all over the underside . . . hundreds in the mouth, hundreds along the nineteen underarms . . . all looking . . . feeling . . . like a man looking for a woman . . . tiny heads blindly feeling for a rock and finding only air. A purple rim runs along the underside of every arm, with paler tubes. Probably its moving-feet.

I put him back in. He unfolds—I had forgotten how purple he was—and slides down into his rock groin, the snail-like feelers waving as if nothing had happened, and nothing has.

A sort of roll develops out of the bay, and lays itself all down this long beach. . . . The hiss of the water wall two inches high, coming in, steady as lions, or African grass fires. Two gulls with feet the color of a pumpkin walk together on the sand. A snipe settles down . . . three squawks . . . the gulls agree to chase it away. Then the wave goes out, the waters mingle so beautifully, it is the mingling after death, the silence, the sweep—so swift— over darkening sand. The airplane sweeps low over the African field at night, lost, no tin cans burning; the old woman stomps around her house on a cane, no lamp lit yet. . . .

I am in a cliff-hollow, surrounded by fossils and furry shells. The sea breathes and breathes under the new moon. Suddenly it rises, hurrying into the long crevices in the rock shelves, it rises like a woman's belly as if nine months has passed in a second; rising like milk to the tiny veins, it overflows like a snake going over a low wall.

I have the sensation that half an inch under my skin there are nomad bands, stringy-legged men with firesticks and wide-eyed babies. The rocks with their backs turned to me have something spiritual in them. On these rocks I am not afraid of death; death is like the sound of the motor in an airplane as we fly, the sound so steady and comforting. And I still haven't found the woman I loved in some former life—how could I, when I have loved only once on this rock, though twice in the moon, and three times in the rising water. Two girl-children leap toward me, shouting, arms in the air. A bird with long wings comes flying toward me in the dusk, pumping just over the darkening waves. He has flown around the whole planet; it has taken him centuries. He returns to me the lean-legged runner laughing as he runs through the stringy grasses, and gives back to me my buttons, and the soft sleeves of my sweater.

Waves rush up, pause, and drag pebbles back around stones . . . pebbles going out. . . . It is a complicated sound, as of small sticks breaking, or kitchen sounds heard from another house. . . . Then the wave comes down to the boulders, and draws out over the stones always wet. . . . And the sound of harsh death waves racing up the roof of loose stones, leaving a tiny rattling in the throat as they go out. . . . And the ecstatic brown sand stretched out between stones: we know there is some resonant anger that is right.

And always another sound, a heavy underground roaring in my ears from the surf farther out, as if the earth were reverberating under the feet of one dancer. It is a comforting sound, like the note of Paradise carried to the Egyptian sands, and I hear the driftwood far out singing, and the great logs, fifty miles out, still floating in, the water under the waters singing, what has not yet come to the surface to float, years that are still down somewhere below the chest, the long trees that have floated all the way from the Pacific islands . . . and the donkey the disciples will find standing beside the white wall. . . .

THE DEAD SEAL

1

Walking north toward the point, I come on a dead seal. From a few feet away, he looks like a brown log. The body is on its back, dead only a few hours. I stand and look at him. There's a quiver in the dead flesh: My God, he's still alive. And a shock goes through me, as if a wall of my room had fallen away.

His head is arched back, the small eyes closed; the whiskers sometimes rise and fall. He is dying. This is the oil. Here on its back is the oil that heats our houses so efficiently. Wind blows fine sand back toward the ocean. The flipper near me lies folded over the stomach, looking like an unfinished arm, lightly glazed with sand at the edges. The other flipper lies half underneath. And the seal's skin looks like an old overcoat, scratched here and there—by sharp mussel shells maybe.

I reach out and touch him. Suddenly he rears up, turns over. He gives three cries: Awaark! Awaark! Awaark!— like the cries from Christmas toys. He lunges toward me; I am terrified and leap back, though I know there can be no teeth in that jaw. He starts flopping toward the sea. But he falls over, on his face. He does not *want* to go back to the sea. He looks up at the sky, and he looks like an old lady who has lost her hair. He puts his chin back down on the sand, rearranges his flippers, and waits for me to go. I go.

2

The next day I go back to say goodbye. He's dead now. But he's not. He's a quarter mile farther up the shore. Today he is thinner, squatting on his stomach, head out.

The ribs show more: each vertebra on the back under the coat is visible, shiny. He breathes in and out.

A wave comes in, touches his nose. He turns and looks at me—the eyes slanted; the crown of his head looks like a boy's leather jacket bending over some bicycle bars. He is taking a long time to die. The whiskers white as porcupine quills, the forehead slopes. . . . Goodbye, brother; die in the sound of waves. Forgive us if we have killed you. Long live your race, your inner-tube race, so uncomfortable on land, so comfortable in the ocean. Be comfortable in death then, when the sand will be out of your nostrils, and you can swim in long loops through the pure death, ducking under as assassinations break above you. You don't want to be touched by me. I climb the cliff and go home the other way.

Lifting my coffee cup, I notice a caterpillar crawling over my sheet of ten-cent airmail stamps. The head is black as a Chinese box. Nine soft accordions follow it around, with a waving motion like a flabby mountain. Skinny brushes used to clean pop bottles rise from some of its shoulders. As I pick up the sheet of stamps, the caterpillar advances around and around the edge, and I see his feet: three pairs under the head, four spongelike pairs under the middle body, and two final pairs at the tip, pink as a puppy's hind legs. As he walks, he rears, six pairs of legs off the stamp, waving around in the air! One of the sponge pairs, and the last two tail pairs, the reserve feet, hold on anxiously. It is the first of September. The leaf shadows are less ferocious on the notebook cover. A man accepts his failures more easily—or perhaps summer's insanity is gone? A man notices ordinary earth, scorned in July, with affection, as he settles down to his daily work, to use stamps.

ANTS

for Jack Maguire

Behind the church in the Isleta Pueblo, there is a court-yard. The sun comes down from the purest ant heavens. On the old flagstones the ants trail after each other, between a fireweed and a rock chip, as they did when the European friars woke and walked here in the morning. The New Mexico trees are spare and detached; wind moves through branches that do not want the fats of this world.

Inside the church, the coffins of the old priests rose every spring. Parishioners stood near the altar each spring and watched. One day a German priest arrived, who said it was only the rising water table, and got ready to bury them again, outside. The Indians collected him one night, covered him with chains, threw him out of the car, padlocked the church, and closed the rectory.

Now the courtyard is left to the ants and the wind, and the priests rise and fall as they wish; a Indian man carries a six-pack of Pepsis across the desert plaza, and the clear shadows falling on the adobe walls resemble the airiest impulses we have, that want to live, and will, if we agree to put ourselves in the hands of the ants.

THE HOCKEY POEM

for Bill Duffy

1. *The Goalie*

The Boston College team has gold helmets, under which the long black hair of the Roman centurian curls out. . . . And they begin. How weird the goalies look with their African masks! The goalie is so lonely anyway, guarding a basket with nothing in it, his wide lower legs wide as ducks'. . . . No matter what gift he is given, he always rejects it. . . . He has a number like 1, a name like Mrazek, sometimes wobbling his legs waiting for the puck, or curling up like a baby in the womb to hold it, staying a second too long on the ice.

The goalie has gone out to mid-ice, and now he sails sadly back to his own box, slowly; he looks prehistoric with his rhinoceros legs; he looks as if he's going to become extinct, and he's just taking his time. . . .

When the players are at the other end, he begins sadly sweeping the ice in front of his house; he is the old witch in the woods, waiting for the children to come home.

2. *The Attack*

They all come hurrying back toward us, suddenly, knees dipping like oil wells; they rush toward us wildly, fins waving, they are pike swimming toward us, their gill fins expanding like the breasts of opera singers; no, they are twelve hands practicing penmanship on the same piece of paper. . . . They flee down the court toward us like birds, swirling two and two, hawks hurrying for the mouse, hurrying down wind valleys, swirling back and forth like amoebae on the pale slide, as they sail in the absolute freedom of water and the body, untroubled by the trou-

100

bled mind, only the body, with wings as if there were no grave, no gravity, only the birds sailing over the cottage far in the deep woods. . . .

Now the goalie is desperate . . . he looks wildly over his left shoulder, rushing toward the other side of his cave, like a mother hawk whose chicks are being taken by two snakes . . . suddenly he flops on the ice like a man trying to cover a whole double bed. He has the puck. He stands up, turns to his right, and drops it on the ice at the right moment; he saves it for one of his children, a mother hen picking up a seed and then dropping it. . . .

But the men are all too clumsy, they can't keep track of the puck . . . no, it is the *puck,* the puck is too fast, too fast for human beings, it humiliates them. The players are like country boys at the fair watching the con man—the puck always turns up under the wrong walnut shell. . . .

They come down ice again, one man guiding the puck this time . . . and Ledingham comes down beautifully, like the canoe through white water, or the lover going up- stream, every stroke right, like the stallion galloping up the valley surrounded by his mares and colts, how beautiful, like the body and soul crossing in a poem. . . .

3. Trouble

The player in position pauses, aims, pauses, cracks his stick on the ice, and a cry as the puck goes in! The goalie stands up disgusted, and throws the puck out. . . .

The player with a broken stick hovers near the cage. When the play shifts, he skates over to his locked-in team- mates, who look like a nest of bristling owls, owl babies, and they hold out a stick to him. . . .

Then the players crash together, their hockey sticks raised like lobster claws. They fight with slow motions, as if undersea . . . they are fighting over some tribal insult or a god, but like lobsters they forget what they're battling for; the clack of the armor plate distracts them, and they feel a pure rage.

Or a fighter sails over to the penalty box, where ten-year-old boys wait, to sit with the criminal, who is their hero. . . . They know society is wrong, the wardens are wrong, the judges hate individuality. . . .

4. The Goalie

And this man with his peaked mask, with slits, how fantastic he is, like a white insect, who has given up on evolution in this life; his family hopes to evolve after death, in the grave. He is ominous as a Dark Ages knight . . . the Black Prince. His enemies defeated him in the day, but every one of them died in their beds that night. . . . At his father's funeral, he carried his own head under his arm.

He is the old woman in the shoe, whose house is never clean, no matter what she does. Perhaps this goalie is not a man at all, but a woman, all women; in her cage everything disappears in the end; we all long for it. All these movements on the ice will end, the advertisements come down, the stadium walls bare. . . . This goalie with his mask is a woman weeping over the children of men, that are cut down like grass, gulls that stand with cold feet on the ice. . . . And at the end, she is still waiting, brushing away the leaves, waiting for the new children developed by speed, by war. . . .

After a month and a half without rain, at last, in late August, darkness comes at three in the afternoon. A cheerful thunder begins, and then the rain. I set a glass out on a table to measure the rain and, suddenly buoyant and affectionate, go indoors to find my children. They are upstairs, playing quietly alone in their doll-filled rooms, hanging pictures, thoughtfully moving "the small things that make them happy" from one side of the room to another. I feel triumphant, without need of money, far from the grave. I walk over the grass, watching the soaked chairs, and the cooled towels, and sit down on my stoop, pulling a chair out with me. The rain deepens. It rolls off the porch roof, making a great puddle near me. The bubbles slide toward the puddle edge, become crowded, and disappear. The black earth turns blacker; it absorbs the rain needles without a sound. The sky is low, everything silent, as when parents are angry. . . . What has failed and been forgiven —the leaves from last year unable to go on, lying near the foundation, dry under the porch, retreat farther into the shadow; they give off a faint hum, as of birds' eggs, or the tail of a dog.

The older we get the more we fail, but the more we fail the more we feel a part of the dead straw of the universe, the corner of a barn with cowdung twenty years old, the chair fallen back on its head in a deserted farmhouse, the belt left hanging over the chairback after the bachelor has died in the ambulance on the way to the city. These objects belong to us; they ride us as the child holds on to the dog's fur; they appear in our dreams; they approach nearer and nearer, coming in slowly from the wainscoting. They make our trunks heavy, accumulating between trips. These objects lie against the ship's side, and will nudge the hole open that lets the water in at last.

CHRISTMAS EVE SERVICE AT MIDNIGHT
AT ST. MICHAEL'S

for Father Richter

A cold night; the sidewalk we walk on icy; the dark surrounds the frail wood houses that were so recently trees. We left my father's house an hour before midnight, carrying boxes of gifts out to the car. My brother, who had been killed six months before, was absent. We had wept sitting near the decorated tree. Now I see the angel on the right of St. Michael's altar kneeling on one knee, a hand pressed to his chin. The long-needled Christmas pine, who is the being inside us who is green both summer and winter, is hung with red ribbons of triumph. And it is hung with thirty golden balls, each ball representing a separate planet on which that eternal one has found a home. Outdoors the snow labors its old Manichean labors to keep the father and his animals in melancholy. We sing. At midnight the priest walks down one or two steps, finds the infant Christ, and puts him into the cradle beneath the altar, where the horses and the sheep have been waiting.

Just after midnight, he turns to face the congregation, lifts up the dry wafer and breaks it—a clear and terrifying sound. He holds up the two halves . . . frightening . . . like so many acts, it is permanent. With his arms spread, the cross clear on his white chasuble, he tells us that Christ intended to leave his body behind. It is confusing . . . we take our bodies with us when we go. I see oceans dark and lifting near flights of stairs, oceans lifting and torn over which the invisible birds drift like husks over November roads. . . . The cups are put down. The ocean has been stirred and calmed. A large man is flying over the water with wings spread, a wound on his chest.

OPENING THE DOOR OF A BARN I THOUGHT
WAS EMPTY ON NEW YEAR'S EVE

I got there by dusk. I open the double barn doors and go in. Sounds of breathing! Thirty steers are wandering around, the partitions gone. Creatures heavy, shaggy, slowly moving in the dying light. Bodies with no St. Teresas look straight at me. The floor is cheerful with clean straw. Snow gleams in the feeding lot through the other door. The bony legs of the steers look frail in the pale light from the snow, like uncles who live in the city.

The windowpanes are clotted with dust and cobwebs. The dog stands up on his hind legs to look over the worn wooden gate. Large shoulders watch him, and he suddenly puts his paws down, frightened. After a while, he puts them up again. A steer's head swings to look at him, and stares for three or four minutes, unable to get a clear picture from the instinct reservoir, then suddenly the steer bolts. . . .

But their enemies are asleep; everyone is asleep. These breathing ones do not demand eternal life; they ask only to eat the crushed corn and the hay, coarse as rivers, and cross the rivers, and sometimes feel an affection run along the heavy nerves. Each of them has the wonder and bewilderment of the large animal, a body with a lamp lit inside, fluttering on a windy night.

The roses lift from the green strawberry-like leaves, their edges notched in a familiar way, for the rosebush is also the plum, the apple, the strawberry, and the cherry. Petals are reddish orange, the color of a robin's breast if it were silk. I look down into the face of one rose: deep down inside there are somber shades, what Tom Thumb experienced so low under chairs, in the carpet darkness . . . those growing swirls of gathering shadows that eyes up near lamps do not see. It is the calm fierceness in the aborigine's eye as he holds his spear polished by his own palm. These inviting lamblike falmers are also the moist curtains of the part of the woman she cannot see; and the cloud that opens, swarming and parting for Adonis. . . . It is an opening seen by no one, only experienced later as rain. And the rose is also the skin petals around the man's stalk, the soft umber folds that enclose so much longing; its tip shows violet, blind, longing for company, knowing already of an intimacy the thunderstorm keeps as its secret, understood by the folds of purple curtains, whose edges drag the floor.

In the center of the nine roses, whose doors are opening, there is one darker rose on a taller stem. It is the rose of the tumbling waters, the strumming at night, the rose of the Ethiopian tumblers who put their heads below their feet on the Egyptian waterfront, wheeling all over the shore. . . . This rose is the man sacrificed yesterday, and the silent one wounded under the oak, the man whose dark foot needs to be healed. He experiences the clumsy feeling that can only weep. The rose is the girl who has gone down to the world below, disobeying her mother, in order to bring calm to the house, traveling alone. . . . And the umber moss on the stag's antlers.

I climb down the bank at Rock Island, Illinois, and cross some tracks. Westward the black railway bridge makes short hops across the river. The riverbank is confused with drifted leaves, chill, the sand cold in late October.

I see a dried-out fish. It is a sturgeon. It is stiff, all its sudden motion gone. I pick it up. Its speckled nose-bone leads back to the eyesocket, and behind that there is a dark hole where the gills once were.

So just behind the head the darkness enters—the somberness under the bunched leaves, the soothing duskiness ten feet down in sand. The pine tree standing by the road-house holds the whole human night in one needle. And the sturgeon holds the sweetness of the hunchback's dreams, where he is straight and whole again, and the earth is flat and crooked. The Virgin brings out four black stones for him from beneath her cloak.

Behind the gill opening the scales go on toward the tail. The dry scales are swift, organized, tubular, straight and humorless as railway schedules or the big clamp of the boxcar, tapering into sleek womanly death.

When I write poems, I need to be near grass that no one else sees, as in this spot, where I sit for an hour under the cottonwood. The long grass has fallen over until it flows. Whatever I am . . . if the great hawks come to look for me, I will be here in this grass. Knobby twigs have dropped on it. The summer's grass still green crosses some dry grass beneath, like the hair of the very old, that we stroke in the morning.

And how beautiful this ring of dry grass is, pale and tan, that curves around the half-buried branch—the grass flows over it, and is pale, gone, ascended, no longer selfish, no longer centered on its mouth; it is centered now on the God "of distance and of absence." Its pale blades lie near each other, circling the dry stick. It is a stick that the rain did not care for, and has ignored, as it fell in the night on men holding horses in the courtyard; and the sunlight was glad that the branch could be ignored, and did not ask to be loved—so I have loved you—and the branch and the grass lie here deserted, a part of the wild things of the world, noticed only for a moment by a heavy, nervous man who sits near them, and feels he has at this moment more joy than anyone alive.

The rubbing of the sleeping bag on my ear made me dream
a rattlesnake was biting me. I was alone, waking the first
morning in the north. I got up, the sky clouded, the floor
cold. I dressed and walked out toward the pasture. And
how good the unevenness of the pasture feels under tennis
shoes! The earth gives little rolls and humps ahead of us.

The earth never lies flat, but is always thinking. It finds
a new feeling and curves over it, rising to bury a toad or a
great man; it accounts for a fallen meteor, or stones rising
from two hundred feet down, giving a little jump for
Satan, and a roll near it for Calvin. . . . I turn and cut
through a strip of cleared woods; only the hardwoods are
still standing. As I come out into the pasture again, I no-
tice something lying on the ground.

It is a wood chunk, but it has open places in it, caves
chewed out by something. The bark has fallen off, that
was the roof. I lift it up and carry it home kitty-corner
over the field.

When I set it on my desk, it stands. The base is an
inch or two of solid wood, only a bit eaten by the acids
that lie in pastures. The top four or five inches is also solid,
a sort of forehead.

In between the forehead and base there are sixteen
floors eaten out by ants. The floors flung out from the
central core are light brown, the color of workmen's
benches, and old eating tables in Norwegian farmhouses.
The open places between are cave-dark, the heavy brown
of barn stalls in November dusk, the dark the cow puts
her head into at the bottom of mangers. . . . A little light
comes in from the sides, as when a woman at forty sud-
denly sees what her mother's silences as she washed

clothes meant, and which are the windows in the side of her own life she has not yet opened.

And these open apartments are where the ant legions labored. The antlered layers awaken, as antennae brush the sandy roof ceilings, low and lanterned with the bull-head of their love. Now the lively almsgivers go forth, over the threshold polished by thousands of pintail-like feet, workers with their electricity for the whole day packed into their solid-state joints and carapaces. Caravans go out, climbing, gelid with the confidence of landowners; and soon they are at work, right here, making delicate balco-nies where their eggs can pass their childhood in embroi-dered chambers; and the infant ants awaken to old father-worked halls, old uncle-loved boards, walls that hold the sighs of the pasture, the moos of confused cows, sound of oak leaves in November, flocks of grasshoppers passing overhead, some car motors from the road, held in the sane wood, given shape by Osiris' love.

*   *   *

These balconies are good places for souls to sit, in the half-dark. If I put it on our altar, souls of the dead in my family can come and sit here; I will keep this place for them. The souls of the dead are no bigger than a grain of wheat when they come, yet they too like to have their back protected from the wind of nothing, the wind of Descartes, and of all who grew thin in maternal depriva-tion. Vigleik can come here, with his lame knee, pinned in 1922 under a tree he himself felled, rolling cigarettes with affectionate fingers, patient and protective. And my brother can sit here if he can find the time; he will bring his friend if he comes. My grandmother will come here surely, sometimes, with the ship she gave me. This balcony resembles her cobstove full of heating caves; and Olai with his favorite horse and buggy, horsehide robe over his knees, ready to start for town, with his mustache; the dead of the Civil War, Thomas Nelson, fat as a berry, supported by his daughters: and others I will not name I would like to come. I will set out a drop of water and a grain of rye for them. What the ants have left behind is an emblem for our destiny, for we too labor, and no one sees our labor. My father's labor who sees? It is in a pasture somewhere not yet found by a walker.

Part Six

Poems from

SLEEPERS JOINING
HANDS *(1973)*

At some time in our life, we may have to turn away from seeing, at least for a while, because certain child parts of us are not strengthened or freshened by our seeing. While I was still writing the *Morning Glory* poems, I felt a longing to compose a radical or root poem that would speak to what has its back turned to me.

I began imagining my childhood by imagining two personalities, one of whom had betrayed the other, and so I started "Sleepers Joining Hands" with images suggesting Joseph's betrayal of his brothers. Naming and describing internal enemies is a practice Blake began for the nineteenth century, and twentieth-century pyschologists have continued it. How many beings we have inside! I know three powerful enemies, who have to be told of in stories such as the Paiute's Stone Shirt, the tailor's traveling companion, Joseph's brothers, Odin's missing eye.

The poems that follow I have rewritten from *Sleepers Joining Hands,* some in minor detail, others in a larger way. The original *Sleepers* line seems to me now too expansive and excitable. The speaker leaves the poem so consistently that there is no one left to hear the feeling that has just been spoken. Certain forms encourage going beyond, breaking limits, replacing the father, capturing the mother, leapfrogging over valuable discriminations, skipping over necessity, outriding philosophical concerns; but there must be compensatory forms that encourage sitting down by the road. The original passages may be found in *Sleepers Joining Hands.*

A DREAM OF A BROTHER

I fall asleep, and dream I am working in the fields.
I show my father the coat stained with goat's blood.
The one whom the grain bundles bowed to goes away,
and we are left alone in the father's house.

I knew that. . . . I sent my brother away.
I saw him turn and leave. It was a schoolyard.
I gave him to the dark people passing.
He learned to sleep alone on the high buttes.

I heard he was near the Missouri, taken in by traveling
    Sioux.
They taught him to wear his hair long,
to glide about naked, drinking water from his hands,
tether horses, follow the faint trail through bent grasses.

In high school I was alone, asleep in the Law.
I took my brother to the other side of the river,
then swam back, left my brother alone on the shore.
On Sixty-sixth Street I noticed he was gone.

I sat down and wept. Hairs of depression
come up through the palm laid on the ground,
impulses to die shoot up in the dark.
In the dark the marmoset opens his eyes.

I wake and find myself in the woods, far from the castle.
The train hurtles through lonely Louisiana at night.
The sleeper turns to the wall, delicate
aircraft dive toward earth.

A woman whispers to me, urges me to speak truths.
"I am afraid that you won't be honest with me."
Half or more of the moon rolls on in shadow.
Owls talk at night, loons wheel cries through lower
    waters.

Hoof marks appear; something with hooves tramples
the grasses while the horses are asleep.
A shape flat and four feet long slips under the door
and lies exhausted on the floor in the morning.

When I look back, there is a blind spot in the car.
It is some bit of my father I keep not seeing.
I cannot remember years of my childhood.
Some parts of me I cannot find now.

I intended that; I threw some parts of me away
at ten; others at twenty; a lot around twenty-eight.
I wanted to thin myself out as a wire is thinned.
Is there enough left of me now to be honest?

The lizard moves stiffly over November roads.
How much I am drawn toward my parents! I walk back
and forth, looking toward the old landing.
Night frogs give out the croak of the planet turning.

I have been alone for two days, and still everything is
    cloudy.
The body surrounds me on all sides.
I walk out and return.
Rain dripping from pine boughs, boards soaked on
    porches,
gray water awakens, fish slide away underneath.
I fall asleep. I meet a man from a milder planet.
I say to him: "I know Christ is from your planet!"
He looks at me as if I had spoken a secret,
then reaches out and touches me on the tip of my cock,
and I fall asleep. How beautiful that sleep is.
I love you in that sleep and pass once more under the
    water.
When I was alone, for three years, alone,
I passed under the earth through the night-water.
I was for three days inside a warm-blooded fish.
A whale bore me back, home, we flew through the
    air. . . .

I was born during the night sea-journey.
I love the whale with his warm organ pipes
in the mouse-killing waters, and I love the men who drift
asleep, for three nights, in octopus waters.
Men in furs gather wood, piling the chunks by walls.
I love the snow; I need privacy as I move.
I am all alone; floating in the cooking pot
on the sea, through the night I am alone.

I call out my wateriness in magnificent words.
That is the water man, but what of the land man?
He lives in a half-fixed house, with plank floor,
where things are half-said, half-sung, half-danced.
Constantly sieged by a power that can't get in,
I feed a multitude of cackling men, who beat
with sticks on the log walls. And when they are drunk,
they fight over water, and spill it on the plank floor.

Judgment

The doctor arrives to inject the movie star against
    delirium tremens.
Hands that lie so often calm on the horse's mane are
    shaking.
His hair hangs down like a skier's hair after a fall.
From a whirlpool drops of black water fly up,
and thousands and thousands of years go by—
like an infinite procession of walnut shells.

That hair that fell to the floor of the barbershop over
    thirty years
lives on in some other place outlasting death.
And those shoelaces, shiny and twisted, that we tossed to
    the side,
live on in their place, and the Hippopotamus horde
    arrives;
the newly dead kneel, and a tip of the lace sends them on
    into fire!

Affinity

I say the clumps of hair weep.
Because hair does not long for immense states;
hair does not hate the poor.
Hair is merciful,
like the arch of night under which the juvenile singer lolls
    back drunk.
Hair is excitable as a child of four or five;
it is a hammock on which the sleeper lies,
dizzy with heat and the earth's motion.

There are golden pins lying in bureau drawers,
whose faces shine with power. They shine
like the cheekbones of saints radiant in their beds,
or their great toes that light the whole room!

Judgment
Prince Philip becomes irritable, the royal sports car
shoots down the narrow roads;
Judy Garland is led hysterical to the Melbourne plane.
The general joins the Jehovah's Witnesses.

There are men who look, and cannot find the road,
and die coughing particles of black flesh onto neighboring
    roofs.

Nailheads that have been brooding on Burton's
    Melancholy under Baltimore rowhouses
roll out into the street under tires,
and catch the Secretary of State
as he goes off to threaten the premiers of underdeveloped
    nations.

So many things are borne down by the world,
by bad luck, corpses pulled down by years of death,
veins clogged with flakes of sludge,
mouths from which bats escape at death,
businessmen reborn as black whales sailing under the
    Arctic ice.

Affinity

I say it is all right. The earth has hair cathedrals.
The priest comes down the aisle wearing caterpillar fur.
In his sermons the toad defeats the knight.

The dying man waves his son away.
He wants his daughter-in-law to come near
so that her hair will fall over his face.

The senator's plane falls in an orchard in Massachusetts.
And there are bitter places, knots
that leave dark pits in the sawdust . . .
the nick on the hornblade through which the mammoth
    escapes.

Aban K.	What you love is gone; the worst have got it.
	The Stalinist shoves the papers to the floor;
	The priest cannot go on with the Mass;
	the singer tries to climb out through the porthole.
Ivar O.	You are a judge; a kind of demon judge—
	the hole in stones through which the wind blows.
Aban K.	Who wants to remain in the world as it is?
	There are broken pieces of wood around the Jesuit;
	the log raft breaks up as it nears the falls;
	the spider runs quickly up the blinding path.
Ivar O.	You want to die, and leap off the earth!
Aban K.	You are a coward to stay and be cheated—
	by landlord and Lord—again and again.
	I suffered for years and you remained in ease!
	I am the strong one; I have endured pain.
	I suffer and do while you go into ecstasy.
	Women love you, not me; and I raged at the start
	from my carrying you. No more. I will blind you.
Ivar O.	Have you put bonds on me? Are you that strong?

IN MOURNING FOR BETRAYAL

I am mourning a murder; one I have done.
I look through the window at telephone poles in water.

I reach for the notebook, and sit up in the train.
I turn on the light; I write out my vows.

The train goes on through Louisiana at night.
My breath grows slow and heavy, in the melancholy.

The betrayer left the garden in the early spring night.
He fed on his own pity, and grew fat on that.

Orrin and his wife, asleep on bare mattresses,
woke; I dream I put my head down between them and
    wept.

Pulling up from far below, the water is born,
spreading white tomb-clothes on the rocky shore.

I see birds below me with massive shoulders,
like humpbacked Puritan ministers, a headstrong beak
    ahead,
and wings supple as the stingray's,
ending in claws, lifting over the shadowy peaks.

Looking down I see dark marks on my shirt.
My mother gave me that shirt and hoped I would have a
    happy marriage
but I have been divorced eight hundred times,
six hundred times yesterday alone.

Morning ends, and the pens on the stove take light.
My life goes by in minutes, in seconds, like dwarf
antelopes in long streaming herds,
or hair flying behind the skidding racer.

No ministers or teachers come out. I am flying
over my bed alone. I am flying over the Josephine forests
where only the rat builds
his nest of leaves, and keeps his mistress in the white
    dusk.

Stumps remind us that resurrection can be cut off.
The sun sinks toward the darkening hills.
My mother's bed looms up in the dark.
The woman in chains stands bewildered as night comes.

THE MAN LOCKED INSIDE THE OAK

One man in me is locked inside an oakwomb,
waiting for lightning, only let out on stormy nights.
At night that man prowls along the porch, dragging
a large pistol, drunk; he has already shot a woman.

Men break doors down on my house to get in.
One moment I am a king, robes brush the stone floor.
The next I flee along the ground like a frightened beast.
In the marshes the mysterious mother calls to her moor-
    bound chicks.

I've known the sad eternity of the cod heaven,
and felt the silver of infinite numbers brush my side.
Infinity has come to me, and I have turned away,
not wanting to carry even the name I wear.

Who is the man locked inside the oakwomb?
A dangerous man; and there is the grief man,
Ivar Oakeson, whom I love so much.
Others false and ghostly live within me also.

Oh yes, I love you, book of my confessions,
where what was swallowed, pushed away, sunken,
driven down, begins to rise from the earth
once more, and the madness and rage from the wells.
The buried is still buried, like cows who eat
in a collapsed strawpile all winter to get out.

Something inside me is still imprisoned in winter straw,
or far back in the mountain where Charlemagne sleeps,
or under the water, hard to get to, guarded by women.
Enough rises from that place to darken my poems;
perhaps too much; and what remains down there
makes a faint glow in the dead leaves.

I am less than half risen. I see how carefully
I have covered my tracks as I wrote,
how well I have brushed over the past with my tail.
Faces look at me from the shallow waters,
where I have pushed them down—
father and mother pushed into the dark.

What am I in my ambition and loneliness?
I am the dust that fills the cracks on the ocean floor.
Floating like the stingray, used to the weight
of the ocean floor, retreating to a cave,
I live as a lizard or a winged shark,
darting out at times to wound others, or get food.

How do we know that the hidden will ever rise?
How do we know that the buried will be revealed?

Some beings get used to life underneath.
Some dreams do not want to move into the light.
Some want to, but can't; they can't make their way out,
because someone is guarding the posts of the door.

Have you seen those Chinese tomb guardians
left at the closed door? They stand with one knee raised;
they half-stand, half-dance, half-rage, half-shout—
hot-tempered muscle-bulgers, big-kneed brow-bulgers.
They scowl for eternity at the half-risen.
What do you have that can get past them?

Part Seven

Poems from

THIS BODY IS
MADE OF CAMPHOR AND
GOPHERWOOD (1977)

I wrote these poems swiftly and heatedly, and they were a new sort of poem for me. When one gives attention to objects, as in the *Morning Glory* poems, one remains in the eyes and looks out through the eyes at another body, perhaps at a starfish, and the mind is focused on the starfish when it writes.

But in *This Body Is Made of Camphor and Gopherwood*, it was as if I had descended into the body, and that immersion is the subject of the poems. When the mind tries to write then, it cannot focus on one detail, because it is surrounded by its subject. Its joy lies in its being unfocused. Surrounded by matter, one sees what is not physical—that is strange. Surrounded by the physical, one feels free to play—that is strange. Inside the body feels like an Ark. Tomas Tranströmer once described a darkened church as a kind of box camera, that gives a split-second shot of something moving at tremendous speed. Writing these poems I saw a glimpse of the Watcher, the Lion, and the Orchard Keeper. I'm sure there are dozens of other beings I haven't seen, and some beings that I did see I haven't described well.

Because of the humor in the poems, I dedicate them to Hermes. Hermes accompanies us to the door of the other world, knocks, and disappears.

When I wake, I hear sheep eating apple peels just outside the screen. The trees are heavy, soaked, cold, and hushed; the sun just rising. All seems calm, and yet some where inside I am not calm. We live in wooden buildings made of two-by-fours, making the landscape nervous for a hundred miles.

And the Emperor in his stone walls called at sixty for rhinoceros horn, sky-blue phoenix eggs, shaped from veined rock, dipped in rooster blood. Around him the wasps kept guard, hens continue their patrol, the oysters open and close all questions.

The heat inside the human body grows. At first it does not know where to throw itself. For a while it knots into will—heavy, burning, sweet; then into generosity, that longs to take on the burdens of others; then into mad love that lasts forever. The artist walks swiftly to his studio, and carves oceanic waves into the dragon's mane.

My friend, this body offers to carry us for nothing—as the ocean carries logs. So on some days the body wails with its great energy; it smashes up the boulders, lifting small crabs, that flow around the sides.

Someone knocks on the door. We do not have time to dress. He wants us to go with him through the blowing and rainy streets, to the dark house.

We will go there, the body says, and there find the father whom we have never met, who wandered out in a snowstorm the night we were born, and who then lost his memory, and has lived since longing for his child, whom he saw only once . . . while he worked as a shoemaker, as a cattle herder in Australia, as a restaurant cook who painted at night.

When you light the lamp you will see him. He sits there behind the door . . . the eyebrows so heavy, the forehead so light . . . lonely in his whole body, waiting for you.

THE UPWARD MOON AND THE DOWNWARD MOON

The sun goes down, each minute the air darker. The night thickens, pulls the earth down to it.

And if my body is earth, then what? Then I am down here, thickening as night comes on. And the moon remains in the sky. Some part of me is up there too. How far it is up to that part!

Earth has earth things, earthly, joined. They snuggle down in one den, one manger; one sweep of arms holds them, one clump of pine. The owlets sit together in one hollow tree. But we are split.

Night comes. . . . Now what? My sun will drop down below the earth, and travel sizzling along the underneath-ocean-darkness path. There a hundred developed saints lie stretched out, throwing bits of darkness onto the road. . . .

At midnight I will go inside, and lie down on my bed, and suddenly my moon will vanish. It will travel on alone over the darkened earth all night, slipping through arms reached up to it. . . . It will go on, looking. . . .

The sleeper will go down toward utter darkness. Who will be with him? He will meet another prisoner in the dungeon, perhaps the baker. . . .

I dreamt all night such glad painful exultant dreams. Each scene was a tile of glazed and luminous clay. What does not have the senses longs for the senses. All longing is terrible and terrifying—a herd of gazelles running over the savannah—and intense and divine, and I saw it lying over the floor in layers there.

All night I longed for my missing limbs. Lines of force at the bottom of Joseph's well sent up lumps of dirt that heal the humpbacked; something rolled upward from the water, became a lion, that prowls around the rocky edges of the desert, keeping the hermit inside his own chest.

THE WATCHER

Inside us there is a listener who listens for what we say, a watcher who watches what we do. Each step we take in conversation with our friends, moving slowly, or flying among worlds, he watches, calling us into what is possible, into what is not said, into the shuckheap of ruined arrowheads, or the old man with missing fingers.

We wake, stretch, stand up, speak our first sentence, and fall as we talk into a hole in the sounds we make. Overly sane afternoons in a room during our twenties come back to us as a son who is mad. Every longing another had that we failed to see returns as a squinting of the eyes when we talk, and no sentimentality, only the ruthless body performing its magic, transforming each of our confrontations into energy, changing our scholarly labors late at night over white-haired books into certainty and healing power, and our cruelties into an old man with missing fingers.

At breakfast we speak of people long known who've left the Path, and two hours later in broad daylight the car slides off the road. I give advice in public one day as if I were adult, and that night a policeman in my dream holds a gun to the head of a blindfolded girl. We talk of eternity and growth, and I pour more wine into my glass than into yours.

THE ORIGIN OF THE PRAISE OF GOD

for Lewis Thomas

My friend, this body is made of bone and excited protozoa! And it is with my body that I love the fields. How do I know what I feel but what the body tells me? Erasmus thinking in the snow, translators of Vergil who burn up the whole room; the man in furs reading the Arabic astrologer falls off his three-legged stool in astonishment; this is the body. . . . So beautifully carved inside, with the curves of the inner ear, and the husk so rough, kunckle-brown.

As we walk, we enter the magnetic fields of other bodies, and every smell we take in the communities of protozoa see; and a being inside us leaps up toward it, as a horse rears at the starting gate. When we come near each other, we are drawn down into the sweetest pools of slowly circling energies, slowly circling smells; and the protozoa know there are odors the shape of oranges, tornadoes, octopuses.

So the space between two people diminishes, it grows less and less, no one to weep; they merge at last. The sound that pours from the fingertips awakens clouds of cells far inside the body, and beings unknown to us start out on a pilgrimage to their Savior, to their holy place. Their holy place is a small black stone that they remember from Protozoic times, when it was rolled away from a door. . . . And it was after that they found their friends, who helped them to digest the hard grains of this world. The cloud of cells awakens, intensifies, swarms. The cells dance inside beams of sunlight so thin we cannot see them. To them each ray is a vast palace, with thousands of rooms. From the dance of the cells praise sentences rise to the throat of the man praying and singing alone in his room. He lets his arms climb above his head, and says: "Now do you still say you cannot choose the Road?"

Snow has fallen on snow for two days behind the Keilen farmhouse. . . . When we put our ears down, near the snow, we hear the sound the porgies hear near the ocean floor, the note the racer hears the moment before his death, the chord that lifts the buoyant swimmer in the channel.

Four pigeon-grass bodies, scarce and fine, sway above the snow. The heron walks dawdling on long legs in white morning fog; a musical thought rises as the pianist sits down at her table; the body labors before dawn to understand its dream.

In its dream, thin legs come down the mountainside, hooves clatter over the wooden bridge, go along a wall, eyes look in at the orchard. Near the well at the center, four men lie stretched out sleeping; each man's sword lies under him. And the orchard keeper, where is he?

My friend, this body is made of energy compacted and whirling. It is the wind that carries the henhouse down the road dancing, and an instant later lifts all four walls apart. It is the horny thumbnail of the retired railway baron, over which his children skate on Sunday; and the forehead bone that does not rot, the woman priest's hair still fresh among Shang ritual things. . . .

We love this body as we love the day we first met the person who led us away from this world; as we love the gift we gave one morning on impulse, in a fraction of a second, that we still see every day; as we love the human face, fresh after love-making, more full of joy than a wagonload of hay.

The cucumbers are thirsty, their big leaves turn away from the wind. I water them after supper; the hose lies curled near the rhubarb. The wind sound blows through the head; a smile appears on the sitter's face as he sits down under a tree. What is comforted words help, the sunken islands speak to us. . . .

Is this world animal or vegetable? Others love us, the cabbages love the earth, the earth is fond of the heavens— A new age comes close through the dark, threatens much, so much is passing away, so many disciplines already gone, but the energy in the double flower does not falter; the wings fold up around the sitting man's face. And these cucumber leaves are my thighs and my toes stretched out in the wind.

So to you waterers who love your gardens, I say, how will you get through this night without water?

I love you so much with this curiously alive and lonely body. It is a young hawk sitting on a tree by the Misssissippi, in early spring, before any green has appeared on the earth beneath. I love you far in my chest, where walnut hollows fill with crackling light and shadows. . . . There birds drink from water drops we offer on the tips of our fingers. My body loves you with what it extracts from the prudent man, hunched over his colony of lizards; and with that it loves you madly, beyond all rules and conventions.

Even the six holes in the flute move about under the dark man's fingers, and the piercing cry goes out over the grown-up pastures no one sees or visits at dusk except the deer, out of all enclosures, who has never seen any bed but his own of wild grass.

I first met you when I had been alone for nine days, and now my lonely hawk body longs to be with you, whom it remembers. It knew how close we are, how close we would always be. There is death, but also this closeness . . . this joy when the bee rises into the air above his hive to find the sun, to become the son, and the traveler moves through exile and loss, through murkiness and failure, to touch the earth again of his own kingdom and kiss the ground.

What shall I say of this? I say, praise to the first man or woman who wrote down this joy clearly, for we cannot remain in love with what we cannot name. . . .

Part Eight

Poems from
THE MAN IN THE
BLACK COAT
TURNS *(1981)*

As I write this, spring rain is falling. The rain makes a careful and reckless sound on the roof of my cabin, persistent as handclaps, shuddery as turkey feathers, and private. Small white tents appear out on the lake as raindrops doubled and tripled fall from the branches hanging out over the water. These white enthusiasms turn in a few seconds to cavities in the water, darker than they were before.

I wanted the poems in *The Man in the Black Coat Turns* to rise out of some darkness beneath us, as when the old Norse poets fished with an ox head as bait in the ocean. We know that the poem will break water only for a moment before it sinks again, but just seeing it rise beneath the boat is enough pleasure for one day; and to know that a large thing lives down there puts us in a calm mood, lets us endure our deprived lives with more grace.

In this book I fished in male waters, which I experienced as deep and cold but containing and nourishing some secret and moving life down below, while waters on the surface are gray and calm. New drops pierce the water and pierce it again an inch away; and the body of the lake lifts and falls slightly, as if in rhythm to the increasing and decreasing sound on the roof.

"Close to the water we sit down one day"—but how do we sit down? I believe that true art imitates nature and her spontaneous sobriety, and that the human being is most artist when he or she has sat quietly for hours near the "ten thousand things" and then is able to carry the precision of their intermingling of watery and hard back to the workroom.

And yet I also love the way human fierceness shapes

raw and open perceptions. Perceptions simply happen, as sprouts or birds appear, but shaping is something we do, and it requires some fierceness. I've often made a net of words in order to catch a perception which had appeared on its own, without notifying me, and which I knew would be gone a few seconds later, on the way to Mexico or Hudson's Bay, depending on the season. But what about a net for the thoughts we have thought for so many years that they are now a part of us—the thought that reappears every two or three years, always fresh, which must be a rebirth of the thought we wrote in our journal ten years before that or twenty years before that? The net for these has to be thicker. Such a thought is not a perception which is happening to us, but an element we are living in; we fight in it as sea lions fight in water.

Reading my earlier poems, I missed seeing in them those thoughts that I have thought for years; and in *The Man in the Black Coat Turns* I wanted to include them, letting them live alongside perceptions that come on their own and the sensuousness that the mind feels when playing with nature. When we speak habitual thoughts we notice they seem soaked in darkness like logs that lie for years on a lakeside, sometimes entirely sunken and sometimes half out of water. What sort of form is proper for these heavy thought-poems?

Free verse in brief lines doesn't seem right, because the quick turnover suggests doubt and hesitation, whereas these thoughts are obsessive, massive, even brutal. And the prose poem form doesn't seem right, because prose poems flow as rivers flow, following gravity around a rock. These thoughts are more like the rocks themselves.

Flowing water takes on form only when it meets resistance; then water shows its drapery-like curves. Form in poetry, too, has something to do with resistance.

Rocks resist being moved, and soul resists seeing itself as other people see it. Words resist being put into meter; language resists being set in parallel beat patterns; a thought resists being asked to ride on seven or eight sounds only. The more limits we set in the poem, the more resistance we have set up, and the more energy the poem produces to push against those limits. When the Anglo-Saxon poets decided on two main consonants only in a line, they were laying rocks in the stream, and the language develops tremendous rhythmical strength to object to that decision.

I aim in these poems, then, for a form that would please the old sober and spontaneous ancestor males. I have tried to knit the stanzas together in sound, and have set myself a task of creating stanzas that each have the same number of beats. To honor one of those old reckless dead men, Pablo Neruda, I wrote a poem in his skinny pitch-enlivened form; and to honor another, William Carlos Williams, I put rocks into the same poem by means of an abrupt line break, placed into the stream at a spot where the language might otherwise flow too easily. When we allow resistance in a poem, we create a poem that seems blocky and a poem that seems as if it could be held in the hand, for it takes on a weight-shape. Such a poem is quite different from a perception poem, or the airiness of our mood poems, and its language begins to take on the darkness and engendered quality of matter.

After a long walk in the woods clear cut for lumber,
lit up by a few young pines,
I turn home,
drawn to water. A coffinlike band
softens half the lake,
draws the shadow
down from westward hills.
It is a massive
masculine shadow,
fifty males sitting together
in hall or crowded room,
lifting something indistinct
up into the resonating night.

Sunlight kindles the water still free of shadow,
kindles it till it glows with the high
pink of wounds.
Reeds stand about in groups
unevenly as if they might
finally ascend
to the sky all together!
Reeds protect
the band near shore.
Each reed has its own thin
thread of darkness inside;
it is relaxed and rooted in the black
mud and snail shells under the sand.

The woman stays in the kitchen, and does not want
to waste fuel by lighting a lamp,
as she waits

for the drunk husband to come home.
Then she serves him
food in silence.
What does the son do?
He turns away,
loses courage,
goes outdoors to feed with wild
things, lives among dens
and huts, eats distance and silence;
he grows long wings, enters the spiral, ascends.

How far he is from working men when he is done!
From all men! The males singing
chant far out
on the water grounded in downward shadow.
He cannot go there because
he has not grieved
as humans grieve. If someone's
head was cut
off, whose was it?
The father's? Or the mother's? Or his?
The dark comes down slowly, the way
snow falls, or herds pass a cave mouth.
I look up at the other shore; it is night.

THE PRODIGAL SON

The Prodigal Son is kneeling in the husks.
He remembers the man about to die
who cried, "Don't let me die, Doctor!"
The swine go on feeding in the sunlight.

When he folds his hands, his knees on corncobs,
he sees the smoke of ships
floating off the isles of Tyre and Sidon,
and father beyond father beyond father.

An old man once, being dragged across the floor
by his shouting son, cried:
"Don't drag me any farther than that crack on the floor—
I only dragged my father that far!"

My father is seventy-five years old.
How difficult it is,
bending the head, looking into the water.
Under the water there's a door the pigs have gone
    through.

Those great sweeps of snow that stop suddenly six feet
    from the house . . .
Thoughts that go so far.
The boy gets out of high school and reads no more books;
the son stops calling home.
The mother puts down her rolling pin and makes no more
    bread.
And the wife looks at her husband one night at a party
    and loves him no more.
The energy leaves the wine, and the minister falls leaving
    the church.
It will not come closer—
the one inside moves back, and the hands touch nothing,
    and are safe.

And the father grieves for his son, and will not leave the
    room where the coffin stands;
he turns away from his wife, and she sleeps alone.

And the sea lifts and falls all night; the moon goes on
    through the unattached heavens alone.
And the toe of the shoe pivots
in the dust. . . .
The man in the black coat turns, and goes back down the
    hill.
No one knows why he came, or why he turned away, and
    did not climb the hill.

Water is practical,
especially
in August.
Faucet water
falls
into the buckets
I carry
to the young
willow trees
whose leaves
have been eaten
off
by grasshoppers.
Or this jar of water
that lies
next to me
on the car seat
as I drive
to my shack.
When I look down,
the seat all
around the jar
is dark,
for water doesn't intend
to give, it gives
anyway
and the jar of water
lies
there quivering
as I drive
through a countryside

of granite quarries,
stones
soon to be shaped
into blocks for the dead,
the only
thing they have
left that is theirs.

For the dead remain inside
us, as water
remains inside granite—
hardly at all—
for their job is to
go
away,
and not come back,
even when we ask them,
but water
comes to us—
it doesn't care
about us; it goes
around us, on the way
to the Minnesota River,
to the Mississippi River,
to the Gulf,
always closer
to where
it has to be.

No one lays flowers
on the grave
of water,
for it is not
here,
it is
gone.

FOR MY SON NOAH, TEN YEARS OLD

Night and day arrive, and day after day goes by,
and what is old remains old, and what is young remains
    young and grows old.
The lumber pile does not grow younger, nor the two-by-
    fours lose their darkness;
but the old tree goes on, the barn stands without help so
    many years;
the advocate of darkness and night is not lost.

The horse steps up, swings on one leg, turns his body;
the chicken flapping claws up onto the roost, its wings
    whelping and walloping,
But what is primitive is not to be shot out into the night
    and the dark,
and slowly the kind man comes closer, loses his rage, sits
    down at table.

So I am proud only of those days that pass in undivided
    tenderness,
when you sit drawing, or making books, stapled, with
    messages to the world,
or coloring a man with fire coming out of his hair.
Or we sit at a table, with small tea carefully poured.
So we pass our time together, calm and delighted.

MY FATHER'S WEDDING

1924

Today, lonely for my father, I saw
a log, or branch,
long, bent, ragged, bark gone.
I felt lonely for my father when I saw it.
It was the log
that lay near my uncle's old milk wagon.

Some men live with a limp they don't hide,
stagger, or drag
a leg. Their sons often are angry.
Only recently I thought:
Doing what you want . . .
Is that like limping? Tracks of it show in sand.

Have you seen those giant bird-
men of Bhutan?
Men in bird masks, with pig noses, dancing,
teeth like a dog's, sometimes
dancing on one bad leg!
They do what they want, the dog's teeth say that.

But I grew up without dog's teeth,
showed a whole body,
left only clear tracks in sand.
I learned to walk swiftly, easily,
no trace of a limp.
I even leaped a little. Guess where my defect is!

Then what? If a man, cautious,
hides his limp,
somebody has to limp it. Things

do it; the surroundings limp.
House walls get scars,
the car breaks down; matter, in drudgery, takes it up.

On my father's wedding day,
no one was there
to hold him. Noble loneliness
held him. Since he never asked for pity
his friends thought he
was whole. Walking alone he could carry it.

He came in limping. It was a simple
wedding, three
or four people. The man in black,
lifting the book, called for order.
And the invisible bride
stepped forward, before his own bride.

He married the invisible bride, not his own.
In her left
breast she carried the three drops
that wound and kill. He already had
his bark-like skin then,
made rough especially to repel the sympathy

he longed for, didn't need, and wouldn't accept.
So the Bible's
words are read. The man in black
speaks the sentence. When the service
is over, I hold him
in my arms for the first time and the last.

After that he was alone
and I was alone.
Few friends came; he invited few.
His two-story house he turned
into a forest,
where both he and I are the hunters.

The Sister hands it to me—the pod
of the sweet-gum tree.
New to me, it is the size
of a cow's eyeball.
Dry as a pine cone, round
and brown. What was soft
in it has vanished,
exploded out
through the holes.
I turn it in my palm;
it pricks the skin.

The spiny protrusions
resemble beaks—hen
beaks widening in fear.
Are the dogs
coming? Where a hen's eye
should be, another
beak is opening, where
her ear should be,
a beak is opening—blindness
and deafness only
make the cries more hoarse.

And what did I do today?
I drove an extra block
twice so as not to pass
the funeral home;
I had three conversations,
all distant. Well then,
if I know how to get by,

why am I frightened?
Lorenzo the Great's eyeball
dangles out, cheek
broken by a cannonball.

The Catholic assassin
strangles the papal candidate
with a thin cord.
King Leopold's men
have already cut off
the black boy's hands, to punish
his father for missing
work; they photograph
the boy's hands
lying on the ground
at the father's feet.

In Nineteen Thirty-eight
Brown Shirts
arrive, smash the contra-
ceptive clinics,
take women away
into breeding hotels.
I look down: Marilyn
Monroe is there.
The arm of the drugged mistress
hangs out one hole
over the side of the bed.

Out of her back comes the Marine's
cry for the medic.

His foot is lying
by the tree,
his lips are open, the sight
is missing—only
the throat and the cry are there.
And the President
in the cold—the white-
haired poet nearby—
lays one hand on the Bible.

VISITING THE FARALLONES

The Farallones seals clubbed,
whales gone, tortoises
taken from islands
to fill the holds, the Empire

dying in its provincial cities,
no one to repair the baths,
farms turned over
to soldiers, the judges corrupt.

The wagon behind bouncing,
breaking on boulders, back
and forth, slowly
smashed to pieces. This crumb-

ling darkness is a reality
too, the feather
on the snow, the rooster's
half-eaten body nearby.

And other worlds I do not see:
The Old People's Home
at dusk, the slow
murmur of conversation.

Crazy Carlson cleared this meadow alone.
Now three blue
jays live in it.
Crazy Carlson cleared it back to the dark firs.
Feminine poplars have stepped out
in front, now
he is dead,
winding their leaves slowly in the motionless October air,

leaves midway between pale green and yellow,
as if a yellow
scarf were floating
six inches down in the Pacific. Old fir branches
above and below make sober
octopus caves,
inviting as the dark-
lidded eyes of those women on islands who live in bark
    huts.

A clear sky floats over the firs, pure blue,
too pure and deep.
There is no room
for the dark-lidded boys who longed to be Hercules.
There is no room even for Christ.
He broke off
his journey toward the Father,
and leaned back into the Mother's fearful tree.

He sank through the bark. The energies the Sadducees
refused him
turned into nails,

and the wine of Cana turned back to vinegar.
Blessings on you, my king, broken
on the poplar tree.
Your shoulders quivered
like an aspen leaf before the storm of Empire.

When you died, your inner horse galloped away
into the wind without
you, and disappeared
into the blue sky. Did you both reach the Father's house?
But the suffering is over now, all consequences finished,
the lake closed
again, as before the leaf fell, all forgiven, the path ended.

Now each young man wanders in the sky alone,
ignoring the absent
moon, not knowing
where ground is, longing once more for the learning
of the fierce male who hung for nine days only
on the windy tree.
When he got down,
darkness was there, inside the folds of darkness words
     hidden.

There is a restless gloom in my mind.
I walk grieving. The leaves are down.
I come at dusk
where, sheltered by poplars, a low pond lies.
The sun abandons the sky, speaking through cold leaves.

A deer comes down the slope toward me,
sees me, turns away, back up the hill
into the lone trees.
It is a doe out in the cold and air alone,
the woman turned away from the philosopher's house.

Someone wanted that. After Heraclitus dies,
the males sink down to *a-pathy,*
to not-suffering.
When you shout at them, they don't reply.
They turn their face toward the crib wall, and die.

A Tang artist painted *The Six Philosophers.*
Five Chinamen talk in the open-walled house,
exchanging thoughts.
Only one is outdoors, looking over
the cliff, being approached from below by rolling mists.

It must be that five of me are indoors!
Yesterday, when I cleaned my study,
I laid your paints,
watercolor paper, sketches, and sable brushes
not on the bookcase, where mine were, but on the floor.

But there are thunderstorms longing to come
into the world through the minds of women!
One bird of yours came:
it was a large friendly bird with big feet,
stubby wings, and arrows lightly stuck in the arms.

Last night I dreamt that my father
was an enormous turtle—the eyes open—
lying on the basement floor.
The weight of his shell kept him from moving.
His jaw hung down—it was large and fleshly.

1

So many things happen
when no one is watching.
Yesterday Peter and I
arrived on the island
to visit Iolani Luahine,
the old holy dancer.
We couldn't find her.
Later that night, he
dreamt he flew out,
saw her temple ahead,
but grew tired, faltered,
turned back, saw me
standing by the window,
caught the balcony
railing, pulled himself in.
I was not there;
instead a woman with claw
feet and hands met him.
She intended to pull
all that he had
out through his navel.
What to do . . . to stall her.
To fight or to flee—
He didn't know. He wanted
to fight *and* to flee.
His feet in tennis shoes
moved back and forth,
rubbing the carpet.
I awoke at four, hearing
the sound of shoe soles

scuffling the soft rug.
Peter was still asleep
and in his bed. When
I called his name,
the sound of shoe soles
stopped. At breakfast
he mentioned his dream.

2

Now I have gone alone
to write by the ocean,
and watch the fish
between rocks.
I feel my eyes
open below the water.
Some power I cannot see
moves these small fish.
The sunlit ocean approaches
and recedes, rolling in
on its black lava base.
So much happens
when no one is watching,
perhaps *because*
no one is watching.
Pirates bring their ship in
when night has come;
the dancer perfects her art
after she performs
no more; the movie becomes
clear when all

the actors are dead.
Earth is a thicket of thistles
waiting for the Wild Man.
Everything is in motion,
even what is still.
The planet turns, and cows
wait for the grassblades
to come rushing to their mouths.

  3
I know there is someone
who tries to teach us.
He has four ways
to do that: First
is Memory, chosen.
I remember that I fell
one Sunday—I was three
or four—from my parents'
car; I saw it leaving
me on the road.
My parents do not recall it.
If we ignore that, he
waits till we are asleep,
opens the images, borrows
faces, turns men to turtles.
I dreamt that I sat
in a chair, and every other
second I disappeared.
That didn't reach me;
I went on with no change.
Then he moves, inter-

feres with matter, books fall
open to a certain passage.
Two strangers in one day
speak the same sentence.
The funeral is over;
the telephone rings;
or tennis shoes
that have no molecules
wake a sleeper.
If we still learn nothing,
then he turns to accidents,
disease, suffering,
lost letters, torpid sleeps,
disaster, catatonia.
We walk, the glass
mountain opens, we fall
in. I usually ignore
the earlier three,
and learn by falling.
This time we live it,
and only awaken years later.

I kneel down to peer into a culvert.
The other end seems far away.
One cone of light floats in the shadowed water.
This is how our children will look when we are dead.

I kneel near floating shadowy water.
On my knees, I am half inside the tunnel—
blue sky widens the far end—
darkened by the shadowy insides of the steel.

Are they all born? I walk on farther;
out in the plowing I see a lake newly made.
I have seen this lake before. . . . It is a lake
I return to each time my children are grown.

I have fathered so many children and returned
to that lake—grayish flat slate banks,
low arctic bushes. I am a water-serpent throwing water
     drops
off my head. My gray loops trail behind me.

How long I live there alone! For a thousand years
I am alone, with no duties, living as I live.
Then one morning a head like mine pokes from the water.
I fight—it's time, it's right—and am torn to pieces
     fighting.

WORDS RISING

for Richard Eberhart

I open my journal, write a few
sounds with green ink, and suddenly
fierceness enters me, stars
begin to revolve, and pick up
alligator dust from under the ocean.
The music comes, I feel the bushy
tail of the Great Bear
reach down and brush the seafloor.

All those lives we lived in the sunlit
shelves of the Dordogne, the thousand
tunes we sang to the skeletons
of Papua, the many times
we died—wounded—under the cloak
of an animal's sniffing, all of these
return, and the grassy nights
we ran for hours in the moonlight.

Watery syllables come welling up.
Anger that barked and howled in the cave,
the luminous head of barley
the priest holds up, growls
from under fur, none of that is lost.
The old earth fragrance remains
in the word "and." We experience
"the" in its lonely suffering.

We are bees then; our honey is language.
Now the honey lies stored in caves
beneath us, and the sound of words
carries what we do not.

When a man or woman feeds a few words
with private grief, the shames we knew
before we could invent the wheel,
then words grow. We slip out

into farmyards, where rabbits lie
stretched out on the ground for buyers.
Wicker baskets and hanged men
come to us as stanzas and vowels.
We see a crowd with dusty
palms turned up inside each
verb. There are eternal vows
held inside the word "Jericho."

Blessings then on the man who labors
in his tiny room, writing stanzas on the lamb;
blessings on the woman who picks the brown
seeds of solitude in afternoon light
out of the black seeds of loneliness.
And blessings on the dictionary maker, huddled among
his bearded words, and on the setter of songs
who sleeps at night inside his violin case.

Part Nine

Poems from

LOVING A WOMAN
IN TWO WORLDS (1985)

In 1973, in the same year I started on *This Body Is Made of Camphor and Gopherwood*, I began the poems that eventually became *Loving a Woman in Two Worlds*, which I published last year. The poems are still close to me, and I won't say much about them. Readers will recognize some poems written in the Blake-Smart-Whitman line; others have a denser, more closed-in form. Love poems seem to ask for every bit of musicianship we have, because they can so easily go out of tune. If the poem veers too far toward actual events, the eternal feeling is lost in the static of our inadequacies; if we confine the poem only to what we feel, the other person disappears.

What I did I did.
I knew that I loved you
and told you that.
Then I lied to you
often so you would love me,
hid the truth,
shammed, lied.

Once human beings
in their way do what they do
they find peaked
castles ahead, they see
lanterns aloft over
the seal-like masses
where they love at night.

The hurricane carries
off the snail, still
clinging to his pine
tree. At night the o-
possum sees the golden
lion upside
down in his dream.

To do what we do
does not mean joy. The sun
rises, and some-
thing strong guides the sun
over the sky until
it carries its spark down
to the northern forests.

In rainy September, when leaves grow down to the dark,
I put my forehead down to the damp, seaweed-smelling
    sand.
The time has come. I have put off choosing for years,
perhaps whole lives. The fern has no choice but to live;
for this crime it receives earth, water, and night.

We close the door. "I have no claim on you."
Dusk comes. "The love I have had with you is enough."
We know we could live apart from one another.
The sheldrake floats apart from the flock.
The oaktree puts out leaves alone on the lonely hillside.

Men and women before us have accomplished this.
I would see you, and you me, once a year.
We would be two kernels, and not be planted.
We stay in the room, door closed, lights out.
I weep with you without shame and without honor.

I go to the door often.
Night and summer. Crickets
lift their cries.
I know you are out.
You are driving
late through the summer night.

I do not know what will happen.
I have no claim on you.
I am one star
you have as guide; others
love you, the night
so dark over the Azores.

You have been working outdoors,
gone all week. I feel you
in this lamp lit
so late. As I reach for it
I feel myself
driving through the night.

I love a firmness in you
that disdains the trivial
and regains the difficult.
You become part then
of the firmness of night,
the granite holding up walls.

There were women in Egypt who
supported with their firmness the stars
as they revolved,

hardly aware
of the passage from night
to day and back to night.

I love you where you go
through the night, not swerving,
clear as the indigo
bunting in her flight,
passing over two
thousand miles of ocean.

WINTER POEM

The quivering wings of the winter ant
wait for lean winter to end.
I love you in slow, dim-witted ways,
hardly speaking, one or two words only.

What caused us each to live hidden?
A wound, the wind, a word, a parent.
Sometimes we wait in a helpless way,
awkwardly, not whole and not healed.

When we hid the wound, we fell back
from a human to a shelled life.
Now we feel the ant's hard chest,
the carapace, the silent tongue.

This must be the way of the ant,
the winter ant, the way of those
who are wounded and want to live:
to breathe, to sense another, and to wait.

"OUT OF THE ROLLING OCEAN, THE CROWD . . ."

It is not only the ant that walks on the carpenter's board
    alone,
nor the March turtle on his boulder surrounded by March
    water . . .
I know there are whitecaps that are born and die alone,
and a rocky pasture, and a new one nearby, with a path
    between.
There are branchy stalks, dropped to the ground last sum-
    mer,
and tires, half worn-down, lifted to the gas station owner's
    rack.
All of them I saw today, and all of them were dear to me,
and the rough-barked young cottonwood alone on the
    windy shore.
Behind matter there is some kind of heat, around and
    behind things,
so that what we experience is not the turtle nor the night
    only,
nor the rising whirlwind, nor the certainty, nor the steady
    gaze,
nor the meeting by the altar, nor the rising sun only.

AT MIDOCEAN

All day I loved you in a fever, holding on to the tail of
    the horse.
I overflowed whenever I reached out to touch you.
My hands moved over your body, covered
    with its dress,
burning, rough, an animal's foot or hand moving over
    leaves.
The rainstorm retires, clouds open, sunlight
sliding over ocean water a thousand miles from land.

FERNS

It was among ferns I learned about eternity.
Below your belly there is a curly place.
Through you I learned to love the ferns on that bank,
and the curve the deer's hoof leaves in sand.

A MAN AND A WOMAN SIT NEAR
EACH OTHER

A man and a woman sit near each other, and they do not
    long
at this moment to be older, or younger, nor born
in any other nation, or time, or place.
They are content to be where they are, talking or not-
    talking.
Their breaths together feed someone whom we do not
    know.
The man sees the way his fingers move;
he sees her hands close around a book she hands to him.
They obey a third body that they share in common.
They have made a promise to love that body.
Age may come, parting may come, death will come.
A man and a woman sit near each other;
as they breathe they feed someone we do not know,
someone we know of, whom we have never seen.

When I come near the red peony flower
I tremble as water does near thunder,
as the well does when the plates of earth move,
or the tree when fifty birds leave at once.

The peony says that we have been given a gift,
and it is not the gift of this world.
Behind the leaves of the peony
there is a world still darker, that feeds many.

LOVE POEM IN TWOS AND THREES

What kind of people
are these? Some stammer
of land, some
want nothing but light—
no house or land
thrown away for a woman,
no ample recklessness.
How much I need
a woman's soul, felt
in my own knees,
shoulders and hands.
I was born sad!
I am a northern goat
of winter light,
up to my knees in snow.
Standing by you, I am
glad as the clams
at high tide, eerily
content as the amorous
ocean owls.

CONVERSATION WITH A HOLY WOMAN NOT SEEN FOR MANY YEARS

After so many years, I come walking to you.
You say: "You have come after so long?"
I could not come earlier. My shabby mouth,
with its cavernous thirst, ate the seeds of longing
that should have been planted. Awkward and baffled,
dishonest, I slept. And I dreamt of sand.
Your eyes in sorrow do not laugh.
I say, "I have come after so many years."

Reading an Anglo-Saxon love poem in its extravagance,
I stand up and walk about the room.
I do not love you in a little way;
oh yes, I do love you in a little way,
the old way, the way of the rowboat alone in the ocean.

The image is a whitewashed house, on David's Head, in
    Wales,
surrounded by flowers, bordered by seashells
and withies. A horse appears at the door
minutes before a storm; the house stands
in a space awakened by salt wind, alone on its cliff.

I take your hand as we work, neither of us speaking.
This is the old union of man and woman,
nothing extraordinary; they both feel a deep
calm in the bones. It is ordinary affection
that our bodies experienced for ten thousand years.

During those years we stroked the hair of the old,
    brought in
roots, painted prayers, slept, laid hair
on fire, took lives, and the bones
of the dead gleamed from under rocks where the love
the roaming tribe gave them made them shine at night.

And we did what we did, made love attentively, then
dove into the river, and our bodies joined as calmly
as the swimmer's shoulders glisten at dawn,

as the pine tree stands in the rain at the edge of the
     village.
The affection rose on a slope century after century.

And one day my faithfulness to you was born.
We sit together silently at the break of day.
We sit an hour, then tears run down my face.
"What is the matter?" you say, looking over.
I answer, "The ship saileth on the salte foam."

THE HAWK

The hawk sweeps down from his aerie,
dives among swallows,
turns over twice in the air,
flying out of Catal-Huyuk.
Slowly a seeing hawk
frees itself from the fog;
its sleek head sees far off.

And the ocean turns in,
gives birth to herring
oriented to the poles.
Oregon fir needles, pungent
as the proverbs of old men,
ride down the Rogue River,
enter the ocean currents.

Land and sea mingle, so we
mingle with sky and wind. A mole
told me that his mother
had gone into the sky,
and his father lay curled
in a horsechestnut shell.
And my brother is part of the ocean.

Our great-uncles, grandfathers,
great-grandfathers, remain.
While we lie asleep, they see
the grasshopper resting
on the grass blade, and the wolverine
sweeping with his elegant
teeth through the forest.

And they come near. Whenever
we talk with a small
child, the dead help us
to choose words. Choosing words,
courage comes. When a man
encouraged by the dead goes
where he wishes to go,

then he sees the long tongue
of water on which the whale
rides on his journey.
When he finds the way
long intended for him,
he tastes through glacial water
the Labrador ferns and snows.

THE HORSE OF DESIRE

"Yesterday I saw a face
that gave off light."
I wrote that the first time
I saw you; now the lines
written that morning
are twenty years old.
What is it that
we see and don't see?

When a horse swings
his head, how easily
his shoulders follow.
When the right thing happens,
the whole body knows.
The road covered with stones
turns to a soft river
moving among reeds.

I love you in those reeds,
and in the bass
quickening there.
My love is in the demons
gobbling the waters,
my desire in their swollen
foreheads poking
earthward out of the trees.

The bear between my legs
has one eye only,
which he offers
to God to see with.
The two beings below with no
eyes at all love you
with the slow persistent
intensity of the blind.

LISTENING TO THE KÖLN CONCERT

After we had loved each other intently,
we heard notes tumbling together,
in late winter, and we heard ice
falling from the ends of twigs.

The notes abandon so much as they move.
They are the food not eaten, the comfort
not taken, the lies not spoken.
The music is my attention to you.

And when the music came again,
later in the day, I saw tears in your eyes.
I saw you turn your face away
so that the others would not see.

When men and women come together,
how much they have to abandon! Wrens
make their nests of fancy threads
and string ends, animals

abandon all their money each year.
What is that men and women leave?
Harder than wrens' doing, they have
to abandon their longing for the perfect.

The inner nest not made by instinct
will never be quite round,
and each has to enter the nest
made by the other imperfect bird.

IN THE MONTH OF MAY

In the month of May when all leaves open,
I see when I walk how well all things
lean on each other, how the bees work,
the fish make their living the first day.
Monarchs fly high; then I understand
I love you with what in me is unfinished.

I love you with what in me is still
changing, what has no head or arms
or legs, what has not found its body.
And why shouldn't the miraculous,
caught on this earth, visit
the old man alone in his hut?

And why shouldn't Gabriel, who loves honey,
be fed with our own radishes and walnuts?
And lovers, tough ones, how many there are
whose holy bodies are not yet born.
Along the roads, I see so many places
I would like us to spend the night.

AFTERTHOUGHTS

These six lines are from Hart Crane's "Pastorale":

> *No more violets,*
> *And the year*
> *Broken into smoky panels.*
> *What woods remember now*
> *Her calls, her enthusiasms?*

The lines are brief and turn over quietly, and we feel a tentative probing that is very attractive, as if the writer hesitates to impose a five-beat line on the reader. Like much other free verse, and excellent free verse, the lines pause, turn inward, allow power to be handled by others. I've written such lines, and yet they do not seem appropriate for political poems. The subject of political poetry is power, and eventually I felt drawn to a line that handles power more directly.

For the form of *The Teeth Mother Naked at Last* I turned to what we could call the Smart-Blake-Whitman line; I'll try to distinguish that from the hesitant or probing free verse.

Whitman aimed at rhetorical power in the sense that Milton, Homer, Shakespeare, and the prophets did. The English line created by the translators of the King James Bible, and altered by Whitman's ebullient energy, is a line of authority and power that unfolds, unrolls, or catapults into the outer world.

> *I heard you, solemn-sweet pipes of the organ as last*
> *Sunday morn I pass'd the church*

Modesty, speech rhythms of others, ordinary conversational pattern, are not paramount to him.

> *Winds of autumn, as I walk'd the woods at dusk I*
> *heard your long-stretch'd sighs up above so*
> *mournful.*

Despite its length, the line holds itself up. Engineers some-times embed steel rods in concrete floors or ceilings so that though fastened and supported at only one end, they stay aloft. The Smart-Blake-Whitman line is flung out from the left-hand wall, and the line, unsupported by interlocking syntax at the further end, yet remains aloft, alert, long-winded, holding its energy, airy as a hawk's wing. Such a feat obviously requires an engineer's cunning, tremendous physical energy, persistent feeling, and, we might even say, conviction.

> *Without any companion it grew there uttering joyous*
> *leaves of dark green.*   (WHITMAN)

Christopher Smart, followed by Blake in his prophetic books, first used it in English; Smart, Blake, and Whitman adapted it, independently, from the King James translation of the psalms and the books of the prophets. Blake believed that public art is crucial to a nation—Michelangelo's mu-rals, for example—and I think we all want poetry that can at times embody public speech, a way of writing that is not introverted.

> *They saw the Serpent temple lifted above, shadowing*
> *the Island white;*
> *They heard the voice of Albion's angel howling in the*
> *flames of Orc.*

Blake describes his line as wiry and bounding, and com-pares it to the line with which an artist encloses a shape in his sketchbook. The line doesn't always drive forward; sometimes it changes its direction in the center:

For in my nature I quested for Beauty, but God, God
  hath sent me to sea for pearls. (SMART)

When I compare my lines to Whitman's or Smart's I am speaking of my intention, not of what I actually accomplished. In my lines or in Whitman's one can glimpse the faults or disadvantages of the line. Its syntax is coral, and grows as coral beds grow; it is therefore quite distinct from the arboreal or hierarchical syntax common to accentual-syllabic poetry. When Shakespeare writes a sonnet he makes judgments on the clauses through his syntax, making some clauses important, others less so. In coral poetry all clauses are equal, which fits Whitman's democratic mood. Its way of growing is additive, and its adding does not show much variety of structure. Musically it is inventive and monotonous. The line often begins in an excitement that lifts the first syllable to a high pitch: "I heard you" . . . and the pitch rises still farther in the middle and then dies away.

Don't tell me how much grief there is in the leaf with
  its natural oils.

The line welcomes prepositions, which English abounds in, and sometimes the line becomes swollen by them. The headlong flow of the rhythm, and its openness to prepositions, means that it may run twenty or thirty syllables without a pause. Smart said of his cat:

For at the first glance of the glory of God in the East
   he worships in his way.
For this is done by wreathing his body seven times
   round with elegant quickness.

The Smart-Blake-Whitman line belongs in general to dec-
laration rather than inquiry, to prophecy rather than med-
itation, to public speech rather than inner debate, and to
rhetoric rather than exchange of feelings; and in this last
quality we see its major flaw.

Alcaeus developed a stanza of forty-one syllables, pro-
viding for many pauses, which Horace and Statius, among
others, later adopted; and an exquisite growth of excite-
ment, slowly intensifying, is built into the form. It's as if
two people bow, and then walk slowly together, watching
each other, start to dance, slowly at first, then faster, then
very fast, then stop at the same moment. In Whitman's
poetry, the stage is bare, then all at once from the left an
athletic dancer leaps on stage, does some dazzling pi-
rouettes, and vanishes behind the curtains on the right. A
second later he appears again at the left, and once more
leaps across the stage, but all such quick entrances and
exits cannot help but call up memories of his leaps earlier
in the performance. The dancer varies his leaps with won-
derful ingenuity, but we are painfully conscious that there
is only one dancer.

The greatness of this line, no matter how rarely
achieved, lies in its initial headlong rush and its powerful
forward sweep, which resembles running animals with

large chests. Its power comes also from the authority of those Hebraic-Elizabethan shouters whose voices penetrated our childhood chambers. The line at other times—for example, at the close of Whitman's "I heard you, solemn sweet pipes of the organ"—proves to be full of silence.

> Heart of my love! you too I heard murmuring low
>   through one of the wrists around my head,
> Heard the pulse of you when all was still ringing
>   little bells last night under my ear.

The line here achieves a Mozartian grace and soundwork that is intimate and delicate as well as powerful.

Baudelaire thought that the prose poem would be the major form of the twentieth century. We know several sorts of prose poems, the most ancient of which is the fable; David Ignatow and Russell Edson are contemporary masters of the fable. Traditionally in the fable, the story is more important than the language that carries it. Rimbaud, in *Les Illuminations,* invented a second sort of prose poem, inspired by the new color separations, known as "illuminations," in the printing industry; there, image and fiery language draw attention away from the story. A third sort, the object poem, centers itself not on story or image but on the object, and it holds on to its fur, so to speak. My predecessors in the object poem are Jiménez and Francis Ponge. Francis Ponge, writing about rain, says:

> *The rain falling into the courtyard where I watch adopts three manners, each distinct. Toward the center it is a delicate netting (or net) often with holes, a determined fall, though somewhat lethargic, and drops light enough, an eternal drizzle with no animal vigor, an obsessed particle of the pure meteor.*

> (TRANSLATION BY ROBERT BLY)

Ponge's diction is precise; he offers language in archaeological layers, drawing some words from science, others from reservoirs of words used in earlier centuries, in order to come close to the object and participate in its complication.

In his essay "The Silent World Is Our Only Homeland," Ponge says:

> In these terms one will surely understand what I con-
> sider to be the true function of poetry. It is to nourish
> the spirit of man by giving him the cosmos to suckle.
> We have only to lower our standard of dominating
> nature, and to raise our standard of participating in it,
> in order to make this reconciliation take place.

(TRANSLATION BY BETH ARCHER)

Among other masters of the "thing" poem, we could name Thoreau in his journals, Tomas Tranströmer, and James Wright in his late poems.

It is easy to start a prose poem, but not easy to make it a work of art. The metered poem, as Yeats remarked, fin-ishes with a click as when a box closes, and the metered poem has two subjects: the thought of the poet and the meter itself. One is personal, the other impersonal. The thing poem written in prose has two subjects but quite different ones; the movement of the writer's mind and the thing itself. One is personal, the other impersonal. While the poet concentrates on the object, the movement of his mind cannot be hidden.

Musicians speak of two possible ways of setting a poem to music. In the first way, the composer—Brahms would be an example—finds a tune, and then uses the same tune for all the stanzas; this might be called unvarying compo-sition. But in a *through*-composed song, as in Hugo Wolf, the composer makes a melody for the first stanza and then alters the melody and rhythm as the poem deepens or changes its mood. One could say that Hugo Wolf sets the movement of the poet's psyche as well as the words. Thing poems then resemble "through composition" in that the focus is not on an unchanging element—meter, for example, or stanza form—but on the changes the mind goes through as it observes.

The prosodic unit in any prose poem is the sentence rather than the line. Despite the difference in length and technique, the nearest relative of the thing poem is not the essay or the short story but the haiku, which evolved in Buddhist Japan through the determination of Buddhist poets to share the universe with flies, frogs, and moonlight. The good haiku is evidence that the poet has overcome, at least for the moment, the category-making mentality that sees everything in polarities: human and animal, inner and outer, spiritual and material, large and small. Issa, a Pure Land Buddhist, died lying in a corncrib during a light snow. His death poem went this way:

> This snow on the bedquilt—
> this too
> is from the Pure land.

(TRANSLATION BY H. R. BLYTH)

The haiku and the object poem are usually written away from the writer's desk, and in the presence of the object. Basho said, "If you want to know about the bamboo, go to the bamboo; if you want to know about the pine, go to the pine." Emerson drew from Coleridge the idea that "every object rightly seen unlocks a new faculty of the Soul." The Buddhists would like Emerson's "rightly." When the human mind honors a stump, for example, by giving it human attention in the right way, something in the soul is released; and often through the stump we receive information we wouldn't have received by thinking or by fantasy.

Why is the thing poem usually composed in prose and not in lines? Lines in free verse or in meter can reach high levels of excitement and emotion which one feels, for instance, in Yeats; the reader flies or is tossed from the emotions to the ideas to the senses and back. But in the prose poem one can stay close to the senses for half a page. Its mood is calm, more like a quiet lake than a sea. When our language becomes abstract, then the prose poem helps to balance that abstraction, and encourages the speaker to stay close to the body, to touch, hearing, color, texture, moisture, dryness, smell. Its strength lies in intimacy. One could also say that in the object poem in prose, the conscious mind gives up, at least to a degree, the adversary position it usually adopts toward the unconscious, and a certain harmony between the two takes place. The gods of the object poem are not Zeus or Athena, but Aphrodite, Hermes, and Demeter.

What is the prose poem's relation to form? I feel that form in art relies on form in nature for its model, and form in nature amounts to a tension between private spontaneity and the hard impersonal. The snail gives its private substance to its private skin or shell, but the shell's curve is utterly impersonal, and follows the Fibonacci sequence. Form in poetry follows this model.

No one can mistake the impersonal side of the sonnet: the hard impersonal includes fourteen lines of ten syllables each, for a total of one hundred forty syllables; syntactically contained thought units, apportioned among three quatrains and a couplet, or an eight-line group and a six-line group; fourteen rhymed lines, and a beat system based on relative loudness of stress, beginning with a relatively soft syllable. The Japanese recognize requirements that make up the impersonal side of the haiku, among them seventeen syllables, a subtle indication of season, and an interlocking and resonant sound.

The prose poem, whether thing poem, fable, or Rimbaudian fire-prose, has no such great tension; it reaches toward no such impersonal shell, and no such hard agreement with the ancestors. As we write it these days, we notice little tension between an impersonal shape it must have and the personal shape it wants to have.

Of course, the writer of the prose poem cannot, despite the seeming freedom, use any rhythm or any sounds he wants to if he or she aims at a work of art. The first twenty or thirty syllables of a prose poem set up, as do the opening syllables of a lined poem, or any human speech, certain expectations felt in the nervous system. For example, if three "oh" sounds appear in the first sentence, intelligences below rational consciousness register these "oh" sounds, even count them, and will expect the following syllables to continue embodying the sound, or to modulate it, possibly to "ow" or "oo." If the writer, ignoring these expectations, provides instead sounds such as "it," "im," "is," the intelligences lose interest, and the game of art collapses. The cat cannot get the mouse to play any more, and either leaves it or eats it. These intelligences hear not only vowel sounds but rhythmic units, consonant repetitions, tunes set up by pitches, and what we could call word-color and word-fragrance. The poem awakens expectations for each of these separate elements. The poet, as he or she proceeds, has then to satisfy these expectations, or recognize they are dissatisfied and outwit them. The expectations don't mind being outwitted. The more the prose poet pays attention to the expectations, the more density the prose poem achieves; and a good prose poem, like a wolverine's claw, can please us with its consistent density.

The fact that no critics have yet laid out formal standards for the prose poem is a blessing. Sometimes a fox and a human being play together best when no loud sounds are heard. When relaxed and aware of no rigid patterns, the mind sometimes gracefully allows itself to play with something equally graceful in nature, and the elegance of the prose poem appears in that play.

I expect that as more poets write prose poems, the thoughtful ones will suggest boundaries or hard agreements that will eventually create what we have called the hard or impersonal part of form. The poets, for example, might reach a consensus on how many sounds the poem will be faithful to, or how the choice of sounds, determined in rhyming poems partly by rhyme words, will be made.

But it is not a genre for beginners. Having no obvious ancient models in form, it cannot be excused from achieving form; with few models of completed themes before it, it still requires completion, and though it has no obvious elegant shape, the reader nevertheless asks it to arrive at elegance.

Index of Titles

Index of First Lines

Permissions Acknowledgments

Grateful acknowledgment is made to the following for permission to reprint poems previously published in somewhat different form.

Harper & Row, Publishers, Inc.:

This Tree Will Be Here for a Thousand Years, copyright © 1979 by Robert Bly; *The Light Around the Body,* copyright © 1959, 1960, 1961, 1962, 1963, 1964, 1965, 1966, 1967 by Robert Bly; *Sleepers Joining Hands,* copyright © 1973 by Robert Bly; *This Body Is Made of Camphor and Gopherwood,* copyright © 1977 by Robert Bly.

Doubleday & Company, Inc.:

Poems listed in Contents and "Night Frogs" from *Loving a Woman in Two Worlds,* copyright © 1985 by Robert Bly; and poems listed in Contents and "A Bouquet of Ten Roses," "The Dried Sturgeon," "The Ant Mansion," "Conversation with a Holy Woman Not Seen for Many Years," "The Good Silence," "Listening to the Köln Concert," and "In the Month of May" from *The Man in the Black Coat Turns,* copyright © 1981 by Robert Bly.

American Poetry Review:

"The Prose Poem as an Evolving Form" originally appeared in somewhat different form in *Singular Voices,* edited by Stephen Berg, under the title "The Mind Playing." Published by Avon Books.

Liveright Publishing Corporation:

The lines from "Pastorale" from *The Complete Poems and Selected Letters and Prose of Hart Crane,* edited by Brom Weber, copyright 1933, © 1958, 1966 by Liveright Publishing Corporation. Reprinted by permission of Liveright Publishing Corporation.

The following are reprinted by permission of the author:

Silence in the Snowy Fields, copyright © 1959, 1960, 1961, 1962 by Robert Bly. Published by Wesleyan University Press.

The Morning Glory, copyright © 1975 by Robert Bly.

The Teeth Mother Naked at Last, copyright © 1970 by Robert Bly. Published by City Lights Books.

"Schoolcraft's Diary Written on the Missouri: 1830" from *New Poets of England and America,* copyright © 1958 by Robert Bly. Published by Meridian Books.

"After Long Busyness" and "Early Springtime Between Madison and Bellingham" from *Jumping Out of Bed,* copyright © 1972 by Robert Bly. Published by Barre Publishers.

"The Loon's Cry" from a booklet *The Loon,* copyright © 1977 by Robert Bly. Published by Ox Head Press.